Don't Expect Me To Cry

Refusing to let Childhood Sexual Abuse steal my life

by Janet Bentley

Nov. 2018

Vi,
Thank you—
much gratitude,
Janet Bentley

Spotlight
Publishing™

Goodyear, AZ

Published in the USA by MBK Enterprises, LLC | Spotlight Publishing™

ISBN for Paperback: ISBN: 978-1-7320727-8-7
ISBN for EBook: ISBN: 978-1-7320727-9-4

Library of Congress Cataloging-in-Publication Data: Janet Bentley

Editors:
Becky Norwood, MBK Enterprises, LLC | Spotlight Publishing™
Laura Wilkinson

Cover Design: Connie Lucas

Interior Layout: fiverr.com/weformat (www.vanzzsolutions.com)

Disclaimer: This is a work of nonfiction based on the life of Janet Bentley and written from her recollections. She has changed the names, descriptions, and identifying characteristics of some individuals to maintain their anonymity. Some of the memories and language shared are graphic in sexual and violent nature. Reader discretion is advised. The author will not be held liable or responsible to any person or entity with respect to alleged damages caused directly or indirectly by the information within this book.

Janet Bentley
www.janetbentley.com

Permissions and Notices

The titles of the sections of this book – Don't Expect Me to Cry, Don't Expect Me to Lie and Don't Expect Me to Die – are taken from the song Jesus Doesn't Want Me For A Sunbeam by The Vaselines and are used in the context of this book with the kind permission of Eugene Kelly and Frances McKee.

Lyrics from Jesus Doesn't Want Me for A Sunbeam by The Vaselines are reproduced with the kind permission of Eugene Kelly and Frances McKee.

The quote at the beginning of this book that begins,
"How much strength does it take to hurt a little girl?"
is used with the kind permission of Fiona Apple.

The quote:
"Our wounds are often the openings into the best and most beautiful part of us."
is used with the kind permission of Dave Richo.

The quote:
"One of the things you learn in rehab is that you're responsible for your own actions."
is used with the kind permission of Dr. Dale Archer.

The quote that begins:
"Killing oneself is, anyway, a misnomer."
is used with the kind permission of Sally Brampton.

The quote:
"Sometimes running away means you're headed in the exact right direction."
is Copyright © 1998 by Alice Hoffman and reprinted by permission of ICM Partners

How much strength does it take to hurt a little girl?
How much strength does it take for the girl to get over it?
Which one of them do you think is stronger?

Fiona Apple on her rapist (Spin Magazine, 1997)

Dedication

I dedicate this book to my Inner Child, to little Janet.

This is your voice, no longer silenced. You matter. You are worthy. You are loved. You are enough. You always have been, even when you forget.

Acknowledgments

Simon, for your unconditional love, support, and acceptance, without which I do not believe I would be here. Your help with this book was invaluable. I love you always and in all ways.

Jeni and Jason, for teaching me what true love is and for being the two reasons for which I ultimately made the decision to stick around. My love for you is immeasurable.

Susan, Andrew, and James, for accepting me into your lives and allowing yourselves to love me and accept my love for you which is no less than if you were my own blood.

Danielle Bentley, for your unconditional love and support in completing this book.

Carson, Madison, Layla, Scarlett, and Adilyn, my beautiful grandchildren, for giving me so much joy and teaching me every day what being present and enjoying life is all about.

Debbie, my sister and Jessica, my niece and Goddaughter, for being my family, for supporting me, for believing me and for loving me.

Mike Gentry, my Trauma Therapist, for the support, patience, and compassion in teaching me how to build a support group and for giving me, finally, a safe place to begin to heal my trauma.

My beautiful support group which includes the most wonderful people I could ever dream of being connected to and who are too numerous to mention. You know who you are, and I love you so very much.

Brad Simpson, my soul brother, without whose love and support, I would never have picked up my writing again and put it into some semblance of order. I love you forever.

To all the survivors of Childhood Sexual Abuse, those who bravely walk this journey of healing every day and those who bravely walked but didn't make it - you give me the purpose and inspiration to keep going.

Last, but never least:

Wil Cardon, my chosen little brother. Depression took you from us far too soon but the short time we had you was filled with laughter, love, and fun. I miss you more than words can express and hope to be enveloped in one of your bear hugs again one day.

Preface

At the end of 2014, I was admitted to an inpatient mental health facility for trauma and severe depression. I was engulfed by darkness with no hope in sight, praying for it all to end there and then. I did not want to die but I was tired. Too tired to live.

Little did I know, that was just the beginning. Little did I know, I was about to start living instead of merely existing. 2014 was one of the toughest and most testing years of my life but I wouldn't change any of it for the world. I am grateful for every part of my life, for the abuse that happened and for every wrong turn I chose to take because it all led me to this moment right here and now.

Today is all I have and the rest will tend to itself.

Writing my experience is part of letting go of the past, letting go of all the secrets that I have lived with for so long. The dirty secrets that I thought I could make go away with my determination but which ate away inside, destroying me with their poison.

This story is about part of a journey filled with tremendous pain. Yet it is also a story filled with the resilience of a little girl wanting to survive.

I write in hope that my survival of the horror that was my childhood will give hope to others who are recovering from or are still in sexually abusive situations. If it helps one person, I will have accomplished what I set out to do. As a good friend once told me, even if that one person is me, it will be worth it.

Janet Bentley
February 2018

Introduction

Abuse is ugly. Child Abuse is uglier still and Childhood Sexual Abuse is the ugliest of them all. The horror is not just in the image of a child being forced to experience something that they cannot make sense of but that it is, in almost every case, perpetrated by someone that was known to and trusted by the child. To destroy that trust and to replace it with such horror and pain is, to me, one of the worst forms of abuse one human being can inflict upon another.

For many years, the subject of sexually abusing a child has lived in the shadows of shame and guilt. People will speak of their child's struggle with bullying or illness but refer to any sexual abuse simply as 'trauma'. Child victims of Sexual Abuse are already deep in their own shame and when the adults around them do not validate their experience, it adds significantly to the damage.

In many (if not most) cases of Childhood Sexual Abuse, the emotional damage done by not being able to deal with it appropriately, lasts significantly longer than the physical damage.

Once traumatized by Childhood Sexual Abuse the victim carries the shame and trauma through the rest of their childhood and on into their adult life. No survivor escapes the pain of carrying the burden of their terrible 'secret' and the catastrophic impact it has on their ability to have healthy and loving relationships.

Survivors are statistically more likely to experience issues with depression, addiction and even to suffer fatal diseases.

The trauma that a survivor carries is an emotional time bomb just waiting to explode into their life when triggered. For many survivors, this occurs without warning and can drive them to deep depression, anxiety and, in some cases, to suicide. Some people experience dark memories flooding into their consciousness – memories that they did not even realize they had hidden away as a child in order to survive the horrific things that were happening to them.

Our society's inability to face the realities of this awful form of abuse, forces the victim to carry the weight of shame and not the abuser. The victim is a helpless child and yet many value what others might think (our family would be shamed if people found out that our child has been abused sexually) over making sure that the child is cared for and helped through the critical early stages of trauma.

It is this deeply-rooted stigma that makes it so difficult for an adult survivor of earlier Childhood Sexual Abuse to seek help and when they do, to be able to talk of their experience. And yet, being able to bring the abuse into the open and tell their story is exactly what is needed in order to begin the process of recovery and to remove the power of the abuser that they have carried for almost all of their lives. The 'secret' cannot survive once it is brought into the open.

The recent public focus on Childhood Sexual Abuse in high-profile cases involving well-known people has helped to make people aware of how prevalent this is in our society. Campaigns encouraging people to identify themselves as victims of early Sexual Abuse have been making headline news around the world. Hopefully, this attention will help remove the stigma and allow people to address Childhood Sexual Abuse promptly and make it unacceptable in all cases.

Good though this publicity is for bringing the subject to the forefront, it does little for the survivor. Indeed, the very publicity which is so important can itself be a trigger to someone who has buried their 'secret' and would do anything not to have to face it.

The best hope for a survivor is to be able to associate with people who understand the crippling agony of 'the secret' and who they know will not judge them as somehow 'to blame' or as 'a bad person' for being abused. As one survivor stands up and tells their story, others will realize that they are not actually alone and that there is hope.

This book, then, is one such story.

Using past journals and letters, Janet Bentley has laid down the story of the abuse she suffered as a child, the impact it had on her as she went through adulthood and the journey she has chosen to take toward recovery and becoming the person she was intended to be.

At times, the book may be uncomfortable for some readers and potentially triggering to others. It is important, however, that Janet details the horrors of the abuse, in order to be able to describe why it had such a lasting impact. This is a book about hope of recovery. It is a beacon of light to other survivors who still suffer the effects of the trauma of their own childhood experiences.

A lot of the material in the book comes from Janet's writings earlier in her life and it is both interesting and painful to read of the emotional turmoil that she experienced.

Janet's writing changes as the story progresses. In the description of her childhood, she is relating events as she saw them as a child, when there was no opportunity to make sense of what happened. Moving on to adulthood and motherhood, Janet refers to her writings of early adulthood when the trauma really affected her ability to cope and the reader gets a strong sense of how debilitating depression can be. The writing of the final part of the book – when Janet starts her journey of recovery – describes deeply troubling emotions but is underpinned by a growing understanding and Janet's constant belief that she can get past the grip of her childhood and lead a healthy and happy life.

Even without the stigma that follows Childhood Sexual Abuse, for a survivor to put words to their worst memories and to let the world see what they have spent their whole life hiding, takes a lot of courage and fortitude.

The book contains details that are as Janet remembers them (or as she described in writings at the time). Janet tells her story as she remembers it. She does not embellish or invent.

Most of all, though, this book gives voice to a survivor. By sharing her story, Janet is reaching to other victims of earlier Sexual Abuse and telling them that they are not alone, that others carry similar 'secrets' and that there is hope for recovery from the trauma.

If just one person reads this and finds the courage to start to face their own trauma then not only does it bring value to this book but, for Janet, the abuse will have been given a purpose greater than anything the abusers could do.

Simon Bentley

Foreword

by Bradley Simpson

We never wanted to talk about it.
Child sexual abuse.
Depression and mental illness.
Addiction.
Suicide.
Now #metoo #timesup blew things wide open.
Now we get ready.
To triumph over it all.

Fact.
By the time you have finished reading this foreword,
at least another two people will have been sexually abused
or raped.
Fact.
If not for this woman, Janet Bentley, and her story, I would
be dead.
Fact.
One in eight young people are sexually abused before the age
of 18.
Fact. Face facts.

An inspiration. A life-saver.
Janet Bentley is a hero.
Not just to me. To countless many.
To the victims, the therapists, the parents, the loved ones,
the perpetrators.
Listen up.
This book is a shocking; shocking inspiration.
A heart wrenching, elevating true story of a superstar.

Janet Bentley should not be here.
As simple as that.
The fact that she is;

is a miracle in itself.
Only reason, insofar as I can tell,
Is that she can stop another from being hurt the way she has
been hurt.

This book is part of Janet's healing.
I know it is a part of mine.
And I know it will be a part of yours.
Whatever you're healing from.

Life deals us cards;
but not like this.
Not like this.
So many wrong cards.
No-one anticipates,
nor expects,
nor deserves,
these cards.
Janet took them,
played them,
lived them,
and dealt them straight back!

Her innocence shattered at a very young age,
by horrific child sexual abuse,
Janet lost faith in everyone
and everything.
Yet she carried on.

Her story will make you sing.
Her story will give you wings.

In 'Don't Expect Me to Cry'
Janet speaks openly and honestly
about things that are almost unfathomable.
This is a true story of triumph.
In the face of insurmountable odds,
without guidance,

simply a determination to survive.
And thrive.
Janet made it here.

I defy anyone.
To go through such suchness.
To emerge victorious
and to live such a life.

Read this book and weep.
And cheer.
Be elated.
Find your own God in Janet's struggle.
Emerge victorious.

This book will tear you apart,
then put you back together,
the way you are meant to be.

A fellow survivor of sexual abuse, I met Janet at The Meadows Treatment facility in Arizona in September 2014. We fell in love with each other's journeys and became friends like no other friends could be.

A fellow victim of child sex abuse, I have found comfort in not feeling alone and been blessed with the support of someone who knows and feels
and thrives
through it all.

From the end Janet.
Until the beginning.
Always your friend.

I thank you for this work Janet.
The world will thank you for this work.

Bradley Simpson

Table of Contents

Part One:
Don't Expect Me To Cry

Chapter 1

"Be it ever so humble, there's no place like home"

Home Sweet Home (song) by John Howard Payne

Family Background

My Dad was an alcoholic, drug addict and drug dealer for as long as I have memories. When my Dad drank, he was violent. He raged and he would beat my mother and/or one of us kids. He was verbally abusive one hundred percent of the time when he drank.

My Mom was also an alcoholic but a different type of drunk. She was very moody when she drank and became an expert at guilt trips. I would feel inadequate because I was not able to help her feel better. She was a very needy person and she needed to feel needed. She somehow made me need her for almost everything.

I required her love and approval to function. The problem was that I could never quite please her enough and I was always left with a feeling of guilt. She told me many times that my needing her made her feel loved. I have since learned that this is a very common relationship issue in dysfunctional families called codependence. I depended on her to an abnormal extent for my own happiness. When she died, I slowly unraveled. I felt as if my soul had crumbled.

My Mom was a victim of emotional and physical abuse not only from my father but from her father as well. I loved my Mom very much and I don't believe she meant to hurt me. She had a very difficult life raising eight children with a husband who was violent and unable to hold down a job. Because of the abuse she suffered, she never learned the coping skills, which may have prevented her from emotionally abusing us.

My Dad grew up rejected by his Dad, abused by his stepdad and in and out of foster homes. He was kicked out of the house at 15 years old and that is when his drug and alcohol abuse began. He lived under the pier at Venice Beach and became involved with some older guys who he took orders from. They were involved in a lot of criminal activities.

He was given a choice by the Court to either go into the Navy or go to prison. He chose the Navy but was eventually discharged because of his drug abuse. He and my mother met in Imperial, California where she grew up.

They married very soon after meeting and I have been told they were happy. I came along a year later. He was evidently very excited and proud of me when I was born, bragging and showing me off. I wish that we could remember things from that age so that I would know what a loving father felt like. I have no memory of feeling loved by him. I have a lot of memories of him being verbally, physically and sexually abusive to me, but none as a loving father.

Early Years / Molestation

From the time I was 4 years old, I was responsible for taking care of my younger siblings. I learned to change diapers, do laundry, cook and babysit at an age where I should have been doing the things 4-year-olds do. I was still a child yet I was responsible for babies.

My mother was in and out of the hospital. At 4 years old, I already had two younger brothers and my Dad was drinking heavily and abusing drugs. I was left alone a lot of the time with no food or supervision.

I thought my Dad was the most important man in the world at that age. He was tall, handsome and I wanted so much for him to love me. I tried to be good for him but being good was never enough. He had demons inside of him and they were taking over his life. They were about to take over my life too and turn it into a nightmare.

While my Mom was in the hospital having one of my siblings, my Dad came into my room one night and sat on the bed and told me that I was going to have to be "strong" while Mom was gone. My younger siblings were going to depend on me to take care of them while he worked. He told me that I was special to him, that I was a good girl and he knew I would help him while my Mom was gone. He picked me up

5

and put me on his lap. I missed my Mom terribly and it felt good to be "Daddy's Girl" and have him give me the comfort that I craved from him.

The next night, he came home late and had been drinking. He was not so comforting. He was in a rage and I was scared. I had made him a peanut butter and jelly sandwich and a glass of milk, and when he saw it, he threw it on the floor. I took my brother's hand and went to pick the younger one up to take them into my room but my Dad grabbed the baby from me and took me to the couch. My brother ran to our room. Shivering from fear, I started crying. "Stop crying or I will give you something to cry about."

He did give me something to cry about. He ripped my clothes off and said it was time for me to "take care of things." Before I could even think about what was to come, he put his penis in my mouth. All I could hear is the baby screaming from the chair. It really hurt while he kept jabbing it deeper and then my mouth was filled with this horrible, thick white stuff and I gagged and threw up. While tears were streaming down my face, he told me to "clean up the mess", which I hurriedly did before he could get any angrier. I then calmed and put the baby to bed. I did not sleep much that night for fear he would come into my room again. I felt so lonely.

This was not the worst thing that would happen to me as the years went by, but it was what shattered my sense of safety. I never felt safe again.

House of Horrors

I woke the next morning and he said "good morning" as if nothing had happened. He said he was proud of me for being so strong while my Mom was gone. Despite the night before, that compliment felt good to me. Daddy wasn't mad anymore and thought I was 'good'. I really wanted to be good enough for him. Good enough for him to love me.

After that first incident, he came into my room regularly, sometimes angry when he had been drinking and sometimes he was 'normal' and seemed caring. He made me touch him in scary places and did horrible, painful things to me. I felt terrified and so very bad.

When my Mom was home, he would still 'visit' my room, but it was less often than when she was in the hospital. I never told anyone about this. My Dad told me it was our special secret and I did not want to anger him. Somebody would always get hurt when he was angry. Most importantly, I really wanted him to love me.

My Mom became very ill after having her fourth baby. She had hepatitis and was in the hospital for a couple of months. I had already started Kindergarten so we had a woman come over to help out while my Dad worked. I did not like her at all. She wasn't there in the evenings when the nightmares would always begin. I wanted my Mom back.

When my Mom came home from this hospital stay, I had lost whatever was left of my childhood. I was always lonely. I always felt different. Nothing I did seemed to make me matter to anyone. My Dad had just lost his job so they decided we would move back to my Mom's hometown. It was close to the Mexican border and very hot. I thought it would be nice to be around other family and perhaps I wouldn't be so lonely anymore.

Sadly, the loneliness and the nightmares followed me.

Attempted Suicides

When I was about 5 years old, I woke up one morning to a lot of blood in the kitchen and living room and my mother and father were nowhere to be found. I was terrified, and with the blood everywhere, I thought my parents had been killed. I gathered up my younger siblings and we stayed in the bedroom all day. I could barely move except to change diapers and get my siblings some food.

Finally, when it was evening, my Mom came home and she told me that Dad would be at the 'hospital' for a few weeks and then we would be moving again. Moving? We had only been in the house a few weeks! This was the second time I had to change schools.

When he came home, he was quieter for a while but, as would become the pattern, he would begin drinking again within a couple of weeks and things would get back to our "normal." My father had several more suicide attempts during my childhood, always ending up in the hospital for a couple of weeks and then coming out right back to the drinks and drugs.

Once, my Mom tried to commit suicide by overdosing on some pills. Dad always had a ready supply of pills available. He abused Codeine, Speed, Valium, and many others. I was very angry and scared after my Mom's suicide attempt. How could she leave me alone with a monster such as my Dad? He was a real-life monster. One that I could not wish away though I had tried so hard to do.

I already cleaned the house, cooked the dinners, took care of my brothers and sisters and tried to keep peace in the house. Without her, I was frightened of what else would happen to us. To me, she was the only thing that kept even a thread of safety and security in our home.

Imperial

We moved to another house in a nearby town. I was not happy about changing schools but I was happy that we would still have family near us. Dad had a job again and he seemed okay for a while. He still drank a lot and it was always a tense time before he came home, not knowing if he would be mean or not.

One weekend, we were invited to a barbecue at the home of one of my aunts. They lived on a small farm and when we arrived I was very excited to see that they had a lake adjacent to their property and a few small animals, including chickens and pigs. My uncle, who I had never met before, came over and asked me if I wanted to see something in the barn. I felt special that he wanted to show me and not my brother, or my older cousin. He took my hand and brought me into the barn.

My eyes were wide as I saw a real tractor parked in there! He walked over to the tractor and motioned for me to join him. I thought I was going to get a ride and that would really show my brother and cousin that I was special! When I walked over there, he picked me up to put me in the tractor seat, at least that is what I thought he was going to do.

Instead, he took my hand and pushed it down into his pants. I didn't understand. I was frightened. I pulled my hand away and he told me not to be afraid and put my hand back in his pants again. He made my hand rub him all over, and I felt sick. Were all men like this? I felt that horrible dirty feeling again that I felt when my Dad 'visited' me at night. I said I wanted to go and when he didn't let me, I started screaming and he instantly put me down.

The screaming had caused my brother, my cousin, and my aunt to come over. They asked what was wrong and my uncle said that when he put me on the tractor I got scared. I did not tell. I was frightened. I was scared that they wouldn't believe me. I was scared that I would be punished or made fun of. Another secret to keep about another man in my family.

Years later, when my grandmother died and my oldest brother, another cousin of mine and I went with my Mom to my grandma's funeral, we were invited to stay the night with my cousin at the farm. I had a violent reaction saying, "No! I do not want to go." Everyone looked at me in surprise, but I still couldn't tell the secret. I was too embarrassed.

When that cousin was 21 years old, he committed suicide by hanging himself. I can only imagine what horrors he must have endured. When I was grown and had my own kids, my Mom showed me some pictures of a recent trip that she took to visit family there. She had gone with my sister and niece and, in one of the pictures, I saw that horrible man holding my niece. She was only about 3 years old, and I told them never to let him hold her again. I finally told her the story and felt so dirty.

We stayed in Imperial for a year or so until my Dad lost his job again. This time, we moved to Oakland, which was a long way away with no family. I never knew why we moved there but what I did know is that I would be changing schools again. I was starting to dread the moves because of this.

Grade School

I became extremely shy and was an expert at blending into the background. I did not make friends easily and, even at that age, I felt so different from others. I had these horrible secrets and they ate away inside of me. I couldn't tell anyone because of my fear, and I kept thinking that if I were good enough, my Dad would start to love me.

I began to have serious stomach pain. It seemed to always hurt. In Oakland, the abuse continued by my Dad and always got worse when my Mom was in the hospital having more babies. I continued to babysit, cook, change diapers and be a surrogate mother to my siblings and a surrogate wife to my Dad.

I felt like I was abnormal and I always felt as if I was going crazy inside. I would feel like I was screaming inside, screaming and screaming with nowhere to go and nowhere to get comfort or reassurance that things would be ok. Things were never ok. Never. There were little remissions from the craziness around me but those remissions never lasted for long. Things always changed for the bad eventually and they could change at a moment's notice.

One minute things would be calm and the next my parents would start arguing about something and he would start beating her. Sometimes she just covered herself, other times she fought back which always made it worse. I remember so many times wishing that she would just be quiet and not rise to whatever argument my Dad was trying to start. Watching my Dad beat her and seeing her battered, bleeding and broken is one of the worst things I witnessed as a child because, as bad as things might be; the chance that my mother would be killed in front of me was beyond terrifying.

The constant waiting for the axe to fall took its toll on us all. There was never a real calm in our house. The horror was never far away.

I was always looking for an escape away from the madness at home. I didn't have many friends because of my shyness. When I did make a friend, that friend became everything to me. I immersed myself into the friendship and depended on it to supply me with happiness and self-worth. It was very difficult for me to have more than one friend at a time. I felt threatened and insecure.

My insecurities would cause many problems in my relationships over the years. I craved love and approval to such an extreme that if I wasn't constantly reassured of it, it felt non-existent. It always surprised me when someone would want to be my friend. I felt so different from everyone else, I felt so "crazy" that it surprised me that other people could not see the ugliness inside me.

I did very well in school. When I was in First Grade, my teacher recommended that I skip a grade, but my Mom decided against it because I had started school early and was already the youngest in the class. Academics came easily to me and I enjoyed learning new things. At school, I felt smart. My teachers always wrote nice comments on my report cards and I got good grades. I craved approval from anywhere I could get it.

By the time I was in Fourth Grade, we had already moved six times. The pattern continued and there was never hope for anything different. The horror became permanent and it felt like there was no way out.

Sharing Homes

The next change of address was when we moved in with another family in Los Angeles, who my parents drank with.

We evidently could not afford to rent our own place. My Dad was working at the time, so I don't really understand why we lived with them as they were horrible. There were 6 of us, they had 4 children and it was a 3-bedroom house. All of the kids slept in one room. There was absolutely no privacy and, though I hated it, I was also used to it by then. I had a constant feeling of shame, the kind that is so deep that you feel dirty and repulsive to everyone.

The nightmare of my life continued there. There were drinking, fighting, violence and drug deals daily in different combinations. Their children, who resented us living with them, were terribly mean. My Dad was never there and when my Mom was gone, I was terrified of the other woman there. Her name was Edith and she fed us moldy bread and green cheese, and if we ever so much as said one word to her about it, she would wash our mouths out with soap. What a horrible practice that is!

The place was filthy and there were cockroaches running around the floor and even into the refrigerator! The kids barely bathed and the youngest of them, a boy, was called "Dipshit", Dippy for short. I felt so dirty and I just wanted to disappear. I wished I had never been born.

One positive during those several months was that my Dad was unable to 'visit' me as there was no opportunity for him to be alone with me.

I found another positive. There was a big empty dirt field across the street and most days there was a man there who would practice shooting with his bow and arrow. We nicknamed him the "bow and arrow man" and, one day, we went over to watch him from the side. He came over to us and asked if we would like to make some money. Would we ever! He said if we went and fetched the arrows after he shot them and brought them back to him, he would give us 10 cents an arrow! That was big money to us and it became a daily ritual. He was there every day and so were we so that we could earn money. He seemed really nice for a man, unlike most of the adult men that had so far been in my life.

We were fetching arrows one day and he asked if we would like to see his other bows. It was just my brother, Benny, and I that day and we were excited. He said they were at his house nearby if we wanted to come see them and we didn't even think twice about it. We rarely had any adults looking out for us so we went without asking or telling anyone. No one missed us while we were gone.

We went into the house and he showed my brother the room with the bows and arrows. He thought it was amazing! While my brother was looking at them all, the "bow and arrow man" asked me to come into another room to show me one that was extra special.

When we got into the room, he put his arm around me. I was starting to feel that familiar uneasy feeling but I didn't want this whole thing to be ruined for us. He seemed so nice and we were always so excited to fetch the arrows every day, and earning spending money was amazing. I let him keep his arm around me and then he reached up into my shirt and as he started to put his other hand into my pants, I pushed him away and ran out of the room, yelling to my brother "we're leaving".

He was clearly disappointed. We left. My brother was very angry with me, saying I should not have left like that. I felt so many confusing feelings. Disgusted, confused, disappointed, angry, and guilty were just a few of them.

The next day, the "bow and arrow man" was there as usual and all the kids went over to fetch the arrows but I would not go. My mother and Edith said I was missing out on earning some spending money but I refused to go regardless of how strange everyone seemed to think I was. I didn't tell anyone about the incident and, in fact, I never told my mother about it. I was too ashamed.

While we lived there, I had never felt so alone and so dirty. At school, I was part of the background. No one even knew my name outside of the classroom. I knew that I was different and not good enough for them. I would never even dream of asking someone to come over and play after school. I was embarrassed at what they would see.

That family would stay in our lives for many years, wherever we lived. I wanted to disappear.

Another Move

One day, my Mom said we would be moving to our own house again. I was so very excited. I wanted to be far away from this family and all the filthiness.

We moved to another rental house, which was about five minutes away from them, but we would live there alone with no other family and that was good! The house was small, only two bedrooms and with seven kids at the time, it was tight. There was no privacy at all and with one bathroom, we were always either waiting or feeling rushed because someone else was waiting. I did not know what feeling calm was.

My Mom and Dad were still drinking a lot. I was 8 years old and still responsible for babysitting the younger children while they went out. I would ask them to get us a babysitter when they went out because I was scared while they were gone. I read a lot of mysteries and true story books and every sound I heard was surely a serial killer!

They told me to grow up. "You've been taking care of these kids for long enough now! Don't be a baby!" One night after they had left, I heard sounds at the front window of the living room. I froze. I did not know what to do and we did not have a phone. I decided to just look out the window and see what it was because the not knowing was scarier. I pulled the curtain back quickly and it was my Dad! He had done this intentionally to scare me because he knew I was already afraid to be alone.

I felt so angry. I couldn't believe he would do this to me. He just laughed and thought it was funny. Then he went out again and they were gone until closing time at the bars which was 2:00 a.m. Around that time, I would begin to relax a little knowing they would be home soon.

They fought a lot because of the constant drinking. Sometimes they would fight in the driveway when they got home and wake the neighbors. The neighbors would yell out of their windows for them to "shut up." Sometimes the police would show up when things got physical. Mom would usually be bleeding and Dad would be cursing and the police would tell them that they had "made their bed, go lie in it."

This behavior did nothing to endear us to our neighbors. There were several kids our ages living in that neighborhood and my brothers made friends easily. I stayed by myself and read a lot. I loved escaping into other worlds that were normal and loving and calm. Inside, I knew I would never have that but I always kept a tiny spark of hope inside my heart and was determined to get out of there one day.

No Hope

I always felt like an outsider in my family. I remember one Christmas, a Polaroid picture was taken of my brothers, sisters, and I opening presents. Looking at the picture, I commented to my Mom that I didn't even look like part of the family. She told me I was being ridiculous and, to this day, I can see that picture clearly. The expression on my face was one of such tremendous sadness and pain. No one seemed to ever notice that pain. It seemed so obvious to me - it was constantly eating away inside of me. The stomach pain continued to plague me throughout my childhood and into my adulthood; it became part of my daily life.

I would cling to anyone who showed me the slightest bit of compassion. I was starving for it, yearning for someone to fill up the empty space inside of me. I clung to many people through the years, including teachers, my friends' fathers, anyone who made me feel smart and important. They were mostly male figures and I would inevitably be devastated when the relationship was never able to replace what I truly longed for – a loving father who cared and was proud of me.

I don't remember ever being able to relax at home. There

15

was a constant air of tension and foreboding. The peace never lasted for long and I could always sense when it was about to end. My father was terrifying when he was drunk. One of us would always take the brunt of his viciousness. It was most frightening to me when others would be the victims. I always wished it was me instead because watching my siblings or my mother being hurt was always more frightening.

I have no memories of any period in my childhood when there was not fighting, name-calling and yelling. In my father's mind, children had no valid opinions or feelings. I was constantly criticized for being too sensitive and I was never listened to. There were so many times I felt as if I would explode with all the confusing feelings that I had inside me. My father always told me I was "crazy" and, as I got older, my mother, brothers and sisters would also call me "crazy." I craved for someone to hear how I felt and care about me just as I was.

As hopeless as things were, my mother made me feel loved most of the time. The hardest part of growing up with her was that you could never tell when she would lash out at you for the smallest thing. She could make me feel loved and cared about one moment and at the same time feel as if I wasn't good enough. I knew deep inside she really did love me but it just felt like she had so much guilt and so many insecurities inside of her that they would overflow to me.

We had a very stormy relationship as I was growing up, especially when I was a teenager. I would be disgusted with her self-pity and wish that she would make things better for us. I never felt comfortable talking with her about anything personal in my life. She was uncomfortable with the subject of dating, sex and anything related. I already felt dirty about all of those subjects so I was fine with that.

When I had my first period, there was no discussion or explanation. I learned about it on my own. I was envious of my friends and their relationships with their Moms. I didn't understand how they were able to talk with them about subjects that in my home were made to be so shameful, something to be embarrassed about. It was not until I was grown, married, and my first child was born that my Mom and I developed a close relationship.

I was very lonely because I was never able to let anyone get close to me. If I did make a friend, the problem would be keeping them. I would eventually reach the point in the friendship where it became too intimate and I would push them away from me. I was very unhappy and didn't know how to change it. However, I also felt a very strong determination inside of me that, somehow, I would manage to escape from the Hell at home. I kept that tiny little spark of hope and I would spend hours in my room imagining the different life I may one day have.

Even though my life at home was consumed with incest, fighting, drinking and constant turmoil, none of my brothers and sisters seemed as unhappy as I was. I remember telling my Mom so many times that I felt something was wrong with me because I felt so sad all the time. Again, I was told I was too "sensitive" and that I "took things too seriously".

What my Mom didn't understand is that I had no control over the sadness and loneliness. It would envelop me like a black cloud and I was powerless to escape. I spent so much of my childhood in my room, alone, crying, and feeling as if there was nobody to help me. I felt so many times that I wanted to die, but thankfully, at that time, I was so petrified of death. That fear kept me from making any serious attempts at suicide.

Chapter 2
"The flames of Love extinguished and fully past and gone"

Auld Lang Syne (poem) by Robert Burns

New Year's Eve

❧

When I was 9 years old, my father broke my heart into little pieces. I have attempted to put those pieces back together throughout my life in so many ways, mostly unhealthy ways, but I have learned that I can never put those particular pieces back together. Ever.

On New Year's Eve, my parents would, without exception, go out drinking. It would be a treat for us kids because they would buy us some snacks to have while they were gone. We often went hungry, so getting chips and dips was something we never got at any other time of the year. They would also leave out pots and pans for us to bang with spoons at midnight if they weren't back by then.

On this particular night, they did not arrive home by midnight. That meant they would be home after 2 a.m. when the bars closed. After we made noise at midnight with the pans, we all went to bed.

I fell asleep and woke when I heard voices, and heard my Mom slurring her way to bed. Then I heard raised voices in the dining area, which seemed unusual this late at night or actually early morning. The voices were getting louder and I recognized one of the voices. He was a regular "business colleague" of my Dad. I could hear them arguing about money and how my Dad owed him for some drugs. The voices got quieter and, all of a sudden, I heard my Dad shouting at me, telling me to get out there. I pretended I was asleep but he came into the room and pulled me out of bed. My siblings stirred a bit but went back to sleep.

When he got me out there, the other man grabbed my arm and pulled me to him. I started crying and begging my Dad to tell this man to stop. He just looked at me with that drugged look and said he needed me to pay a debt.

I started sobbing; begging my Dad to intervene while this man slapped me across the face, telling me to shut up. He dragged me to the living area, which was in full view of my Dad and ripped my clothes off. Even though my Dad had, by this time, molested me so often, I felt such shame at being exposed in front of him that way. It was a type of shame that was worse than I had ever felt before.

He took his pants off but left his shirt on. He crouched over me and as I was waiting for my mouth to be gagged with this horrible man's penis, he instead wrenched my legs apart. I was trembling with a greater fear than I ever remembered feeling. I tried to put my legs back together but he just wrenched them apart further. He then raped me. I thought I was going to die. The pain was unbearable. I screamed and tried to get away from him, but he held me down and slapped me again and again, telling me to stop.

Where was my Mom? I was sure that my siblings must have been hearing this. Why didn't anyone help me?

All of a sudden, he grunted and I felt so much liquid between my legs. He got up and went to sit at the table with my Dad. My Dad did not get up to help me, he did not tell me he was sorry, he just told me to clean up and go back to bed.

When I sat up, my legs were covered with semen and blood. I understood the semen by then but I did not understand where all the blood was coming from and it really frightened me. I was in so much pain that I could barely stand up. I went into the bathroom and tried to clean up as best as I could. I scrubbed and scrubbed until every drop was gone, but I still didn't feel clean, so I kept scrubbing until I was raw.

Afterwards, laying back in bed in the same room as my siblings, I made a conscious decision that I would stop crying. I would pretend like I was not there. It was similar to when my Dad molested me and I would go places in my mind, but this time, it was more intense. I was able to shut down the hurt and pain inside and feel nothing. My mind went white and while I was there, I didn't have to think. I didn't have to relive anything. I didn't have to exist in the present. I stayed that way for a few hours until I was too exhausted to keep my eyes open.

I woke up the next morning wishing I could die. I did not want to be here anymore. I wanted to be in that white, numb place all the time. I did not want to feel.

Chapter 3

"Sunbeams are not made like me"

Jesus Doesn't Want Me For A Sunbeam (song) by
The Vaselines

Religion

Two wonderful things happened when I was 11 years old. I started menstruating, which caused my Dad to stay away from me, and a new family moved to our neighborhood.

There were two girls; one of them was my age and we became friends. She was the first real friend I had ever had. Usually, the parents of children living near us or at school would not allow their children to come over to our house and play. In retrospect, although it was very lonely, it was the best thing for them.

My first friend's name was Kathleen but I called her Kath. She seemed very kind, her parents seemed the same, and in my child's view, "normal", unlike our family. I began to spend time at her house playing and having sleepovers. There was no fighting and no name-calling, just kindness.

As I got to know her, she told me that her and her family went to a Church in the next town over. They attended services on Sunday mornings and evenings, Wednesday and Friday evenings and she asked if I wanted to come with them sometime. I thought it sounded fun and it would allow me not only more time with her, but time away from the madness at home.

The first time I went with her was a Sunday and we started off in small Sunday School classes grouped by age. The Pastor's daughters were my age also and there were about nine of us in the class. I loved it. I enjoyed regular school and this was similar. I was a sponge, soaking up anything and everything I could. After Sunday School, we then went up to the main Church with all the adults for the morning service. There were a lot of normal looking people and they all seemed welcoming and kind. I was a bit embarrassed because they were all dressed so nicely and my clothes were always too small and usually very tattered, but they didn't seem to notice.

Several songs were sung by the congregation and the Pastor's daughter played the piano up on the platform where her Dad sat. I was scared at first by the actions of the congregation. Everyone was clapping hands, raising their hands, shouting out "Thank you Lord" and "Praise God" and similar things. A few of them seemed to be speaking in a different language.

After the songs, it was time for testimonies. People would randomly stand up and thank God for different things. Every once in a while, someone would stand up to "testify" and break out into that different language and they looked like they were having little seizures as they spoke. Most times, after this happened, another person would jump up and "translate" what had been said in the other language.

Sometimes it would be nice things and sometimes it would be about scary things. There would be warnings from God to follow the Church rules and to do everything you could to save outside people (sinners) from Hell. If you did not spread the word to the sinners, then you would go to Hell, a fire and brimstone place with a devil that punished you. I had never heard of this before. My Mom had always told me that if I believed in God, I would go to Heaven so this was a new concept to me.

Next, it was time for the Pastor to give the sermon. He read different verses from the Bible and then spoke about what God meant by them and how they applied to us as His servants. Again, there was always a type of warning in the sermon and an admonition to either do or not do certain "worldly" things if you wanted to go to Heaven. I felt scared but curious and it was such a different environment from home. There were people who seemed nice to me, who seemed to care and that was like water to someone dying of thirst.

After Church services, Kath's family usually went out to eat lunch at a restaurant with some other members of the Church. It was a regular thing, and I was invited on this first Sunday. I had only been in a restaurant twice in my life before then and I loved it. I felt so special and so happy to feel part of a 'normal' family. There was love and discipline and conversation without yelling. It was all a bit overwhelming, but in a good way.

Rules

After that Sunday, I went to Church with them every chance I could. There were two services on Sundays, a Wednesday evening service, and Friday evening youth services. It was like a miracle to have this place to go and to have these people who cared!

Kath's father was the Assistant Pastor of the Church and sometimes delivered sermons. He also spent Saturdays at the Church doing whatever Assistant Pastors did. We went with him one Saturday. Kath and I were becoming best friends by then.

While we were playing outside, the Pastor came out from the Church and when he saw us, he came over. He looked at me and said that he did not approve of what I was wearing and that if I wanted to return to the Church, I would have to comply with the dress code. I didn't know what he meant and when he walked away, Kath told me that he was talking about the sleeves on my dress. They were short sleeves above my elbows and, evidently, females were only allowed to wear clothing with sleeves below the elbow.

I instantly felt shame and embarrassment. The Pastor, the leader of the Church, did not like me. At least that is what that little girl thought. I felt so rejected as I had just wanted to fit in with these people who were so kind.

Kath continued to tell me some of the other rules of the Church that had to be followed if I wanted to keep attending. Girls must wear dresses below their knees (no trousers allowed of any sort, including shorts), sleeves of all clothing must be below the elbow and girls could not cut their hair, even for a trim. There was no removing of any hair, including plucking eyebrows and shaving of any kind. There was no jewelry allowed and no listening to anything but Church music (other music was called 'worldly' music). There was so much more that I would learn later but this was enough to make me feel uneasy.

When I got home later that day, I told my Mom that the Church had rules about what to wear and do. My Dad started laughing. He said that I was already crazy, and now I would be crazier. In retrospect, I think my Mom knew that my involvement with my friend, her family and now this Church was a way for me to escape home and she did not say anything about it.

All I believed at the time was that to be accepted by these people, this Church and by God, I must obey these rules and I planned to do that! I did not want to go to a place of fire and brimstone, which sounded scarier even than my life at home because it was forever and there would be no spark of hope at all.

Later in my life, I learned about 'Religious abuse', which refers to abuse administered under the guise of religion, including harassment or humiliation, resulting in psychological trauma. Religious abuse may also include misuse of religion for selfish, secular or ideological ends. Some religions build up your trust and dependence in their doctrine to a point that you would do anything for them, anything.

At the time, of course, I had no knowledge of such things. Even with the 'rules', the Church was a refuge from the chaos of home

I followed the rules the best I could. If I didn't have any dresses with long sleeves, I would wear a long sleeve shirt underneath and I made sure any dress or skirt I wore was below my knees. One time, I wore a shorter skirt pulled way down and a long shirt to cover it just so that I complied. After a while, Kath's Mom, who sewed, made me a few dresses. They were maxi dresses and went all the way to the floor and they were NEW! They smelled new and I loved it. In Junior High School, I took a sewing class and learned how to sew my own clothes. I saved every penny I could to buy materials to make clothes.

I continued to go to this Church and felt like I belonged there and that I was doing all the right things to please God and to be able to get into Heaven. Things at home were the same. Drinking, drugging, fighting, and craziness. I was so happy I had this place to go to and escape all of it.

Another Move and Baby

When I was 12 years old, we moved to another house a couple of blocks over. My Mom had become pregnant again, and she had my brother shortly after we moved. Things were different this time. She and my Dad seemed very worried and told us that there was a problem with the new baby.

My mother talked to me one day about my new brother, Martin, and explained that he had complications when he was born and that he would be different. Later, I learned that he had a form of Palsy but at the time, I just said, "I don't care, I will love him and take care of him." She then went on to say that he would have special needs and would need special equipment and a lot of surgeries. To me, it didn't matter.

Martin pretty much lived in and out of the Children's Hospital in Los Angeles. He had numerous surgeries and was required to wear a helmet to protect his delicate head. He had seizures that were scary and he took special medication for them.

There was a significant change in the household environment. My mother was always away from home. She was at the hospital, doctor appointments or special events that were sponsored for children with special needs. She was far too busy and stressed to be there for anything else. I was often in the house alone with my Dad and my siblings. He was still drinking and drugging; constantly drunk, smoking pot, and using other drugs.

I was worried that I would lose my friend, Kath, but she remained my friend. I needed her to stay with me. If she left,

I felt I would die. I would have no friends. I continued going to the Church services with her and her family. They would now drive over and pick me up from our new house. The new house was much better. It had 3 bedrooms and an extra room off the kitchen that had no door but served as a much-needed bedroom.

I prayed that the ever-present cockroaches that had followed us from that other family would go away now that we were at our new place, but they became worse. They were everywhere. They would crawl on the floors when a light was turned on. They would fly at times, which was terrifying. They would sometimes be in the beds and, worst of all, they were all over the kitchen and would get through the cracks into the refrigerator.

It was like living in a horror film and I began to offer to do all the cooking because at least I could make sure everything was clean. I would not eat leftovers unless I was extra-hungry because I knew the bugs had probably crawled all over them. I was too embarrassed to bring Kath over because of it. It was another thing that I wanted to hide and keep secret.

While all of this was happening, the members of the Church were relentlessly telling me that I needed to "get my parents to the Church" so they could be "saved." It was the last thing that I wanted. This was MY place. This was MY home away from home and I could be a "normal" person here.

Dirty Secrets

There were youth activities at the Church that we were able to participate in - going to the snow, attending Summer Camp and traveling to revivals at other Churches. The oppressive Fundamentalist religion was the only true Church according to our Pastor, who received his interpretations of the Bible straight from God. All the other religions were false and if you ever left this Church and attended another, you were a backslider and would go to Hell.

The revivals were normal Church services on a bigger scale, held in the hope that more people would attend and be saved. When I was 12 years old, there was an overnight revival that I will never forget. They were usually fun events because we got to travel in the Church bus together, even stay in a motel, and it was like a mini vacation for me.

On this occasion, we arrived at the motel with the adults as our chaperones, unpacked and headed out to the service. By this time, I had made another friend who attended Church with her mother and siblings. She had an older brother, Brady, who was a Senior in High School, and a younger brother who would hang out with us when I had sleepovers at her house.

We returned to the hotel that night after the service and, as we were getting off of the bus, Brady whispered to me to meet him an hour later at the swimming pool area. I felt SO flattered. All the older girls had a crush on him and he wanted ME to meet him. I was on "cloud nine" the entire time that I was lying in bed waiting for that hour to pass and for Kath to fall asleep.

When it was time, I snuck out of the room and when I arrived at the pool, he was waiting for me. He said he liked me a lot. I was extremely shy and just smiled. He came over to me, pulled me to him and started kissing me. My guard went up, but this felt different. This was the real deal, tongues and everything and wow it felt good and my hormones were happy! I could have kissed him like that forever. I had only ever had other things shoved in my mouth but I had never been kissed.

Suddenly, he pulled up my dress and put his hands in my panties. I didn't like that. I had been in this situation before and I was scared. I tried to pull away but he got angry and wouldn't let me. He was very strong. He stuck his fingers inside me and it hurt as he kept pushing further and deeper. He took them out and held me with one hand, stuck his tongue in my mouth while touching himself. By this time, I knew exactly what was coming. He ejaculated and pushed my face down there and told me to clean up or he would hurt me. I did what he said while my mind went elsewhere, and then he walked away, turned around and said that if I told anyone, he would deny it and people would know I was lying.

I felt another part of my heart crumble and I went back to my room feeling filthy and unloved. I thought to myself that he was going to get into big trouble and surely this would not be allowed in this religion. It couldn't be. The next morning, while getting ready for the day, I told Kath about it. She did not seem to be shocked which was curious to me but I didn't question it and she advised me to tell his older sister, Mary, who was there as a chaperone. She seemed kind and was always very strict in the religion, always testifying during the services, always doing everything "right".

I went to her and asked if I could speak to her alone. She came into my room and although she seemed impatient, I told her what had happened and waited for her to offer me some help or protection from the situation. She looked at me and calmly said that I was a liar and that if I ever told anyone about this, she would make sure they knew I was lying. She then left, leaving me alone with my thoughts and my fear and my shame. There was no one I could talk to about this. I would be called a liar and shamed. Was I going to lose my place in this Church? I would be left with nothing but the horribleness of my family life. So, I kept my mouth shut. Another secret to keep inside.

We left on the bus later that day to go home and, while we were on the bus, no one spoke to me. No one. Not even Kath. It felt like everyone was mad at me and knew what had happened. Word had spread. I felt that everyone was thinking how dirty I was to make up such a lie. I felt completely shunned by all of them and, when I got home, I felt more alone than at any other time in my life. I felt that I had ruined what was the only outside life I had found to escape from home.

Kath came over a few days later and asked if I wanted

to come to her house to hang out and I jumped at the opportunity. We were friends again as if nothing had ever happened. Nothing was said about the Revival event. I went to Church with her and although I felt very self-conscious thinking everyone would be angry with me, they acted like nothing had happened. Brady completely ignored me and pursued the Pastor's daughter. They started "going together" as it was called then when you were a couple and every once in a while he would give me a secret smile, reminding me of my place.

Life Continues

Life went on and things were worse at home. My Dad was drinking more than ever, my Mom was now drinking heavily and I was left alone more and more with the younger kids. My Dad constantly made fun of me, either for what I was wearing or how I was feeling. I would try so hard to look nice but I would either be a "freak" or a "whore". He was out of a job again, and he and Mom fought more and more often.

He started beating her outside in public. She was usually drunk too and so they would fight until there was blood. The neighbors watched and not one of them came to help. They knew us and, looking back on it, I suppose they were used to it. When these fights would happen, I would scream for them to stop, which would be futile. I would take my younger siblings into the bedroom and read to them, trying to keep the fear and the noise away from them.

I was never as ashamed as I was during this period. It seemed worse than when it happened at the other houses because my now best friend and her family had witnessed it and I was so embarrassed to have our life out in the open where everyone could see it.

Kath's family must have been telling the Pastor of the Church about my home situation because the focus with them and the Church became to "save" my family. Being "saved" was defined as attending Church, receiving the Holy Ghost (evidenced by speaking in tongues) and being baptized, after which you would follow all rules of the Church and go to Heaven.

I had a big problem with their attempt to bring my family to the Church because, as I said, I did not want them there! I could not share this with anyone. It was mine. It was my outside life. It was my escape and, even with all of the negatives, it was comfort to me. Thus began my long habit of lying about my family and my home. When I was asked if I had invited my parents to Church, I said "yes." I told my friend, my friend's family and the Church members who asked me about it that they did not want to come. I was embarrassed about my real life. I wanted this pretend life so that I could feel okay at least part of the time.

One Sunday morning, the Pastor stopped during the sermon and started "speaking in tongues" which I had eventually learned was the name of the different language. It was a language of God speaking through a human to get a message delivered. When he was finished, my friend's Mom jumped up and began translating. God had told her that someone in the congregation today was embarrassed to bring their family to Church. God loved everybody and that preventing this from happening was the work of the devil and would be punished. My face must have turned beet red. Everyone looked at me and everyone knew who she was talking about. I felt evil like the scum of the earth that, deep inside, I knew I really was.

I was grateful when the sermon was over and as I was walking out the door, the Pastor asked me if I would be bringing my parents to Church for the evening service. I said I would try. Another lie. That evening, I could sense the disappointment that the Pastor and the congregation felt when my parents were not with me. The Pastor came up to me after the service and said God was very disappointed in me and that I was not following His message. More shame.

I was very confused. I felt like there was no acceptance of me anywhere. I was always told I was not good enough from someone and I felt very damaged inside. However, the horrors at home were worse than this environment so I continued to strive to follow all the rules and trying so hard to be good enough for this Church and its congregation that I needed to believe in so desperately.

Dad and Church

One Sunday night during the middle of the sermon, the double doors at the entrance to the Church opened. Everyone turned around to see who it was. To my absolute horror and embarrassment, it was my Dad and he was drunk, very drunk.

The elders of the Church came to guide him to the front pew to sit. As he was staggering down the aisle, he turned around and started calling out "Where is Janet?" I wanted to sink into the floor, not only out of embarrassment but out of fear. He started saying things like "she doesn't want me here" and "she is embarrassed of me". At the end of the services, there was always an invitation to come to the altar at the front to pray and ask to be saved and to be "filled with the Holy Ghost." My Dad went down to be saved and the men were all around him anointing him with oil and praying for him.

After the service, I was shunned again. I should be ashamed of myself for not helping my Dad and going to sit by him. My friend's family did not let me drive home with them that evening, saying I should go home with my Dad (I guess drunk driving wasn't as big of an issue then as it is now). I felt abandoned and scared.

In the car with my Dad, he started shouting at me, telling me that I should have welcomed him instead of being embarrassed that he came. This was from the man who had, by this time, molested me since the age of four and had ridiculed me every day of my life.

Uncontrollably angry, he pulled over to the side of the road and started beating me with his belt. It was a station

34

wagon and he put me in the back, laid me down, told me to turn over and beat me until I bled. When I tried to cover myself with my arms, he would push me down again on my stomach so I couldn't turn over. I remember only crying a little bit because, by this time, I was an expert at dissociating. I would go numb and see nothing in my mind. I would cease to be.

When we got home, it was very late and everyone was in bed. I went straight to bed after being told to wear a sweater until the cuts and bruises healed. I was so afraid of him that I would do anything he said. I still returned to the Church at the next scheduled service because I had nowhere else to go to get away from home. When I was asked where my Dad was, I told them he did not want to come back. They walked away like they didn't believe me, and though I felt so much shame, I kept coming back.

Junior High School

While I was attending Junior High School, the rules of the Church were an additional source of embarrassment. They required us to wear dresses below the knees, sleeves below the elbows and no trousers or shorts. We had to wear special clothing for gym class. We were excused for religious beliefs and allowed to wear a special modest shirt and culottes, which was a skirt below our knees with a split in the middle.

Of course, we were made fun of by our peers and endured horrible bullying which made me feel even more ostracized. The Church told us that this "persecution" was part of standing up for the principles of the religion and Jesus Christ.

Chapter 4

"Brothers and sisters are as close as hands and feet."

Vietnamese Proverb

Brothers in arms

I became a loner in Junior High and High School. I earned a 4.0 grade point average and won a scholarship to college but never told my parents. I didn't want to draw attention to myself in any way for fear it would cause more disappointment.

Around this time, three of my brothers and one of my sisters were experimenting with drugs, smoking and ditching school on a regular basis. Because my Dad was still into heavy drugs, they were readily available with the dealers in and out of our house constantly.

My eldest brother had such an innocent face. He had freckles like I did and a cute little face. He was my protector. One day, as I walked to the bus stop for school, I took a shortcut down the alley at the end of our block. I usually walked with him but he had left before me that day. As I was walking, a white car came up behind me and was driving really slowly. I knew this was not good.

I walked faster but the car caught up to the side of me. The window rolled down and there were two men in the front asking if I wanted a ride. I said "no" and when one of them started to open the door, I started running. I got to the end of the alley before they caught up with me and it was too public for them to be able to grab me.

I was out of breath by the time I got to the bus stop and my brother instantly asked what happened. When I told him, he took off running back to the alley. What makes this memory so special to me is that he was just a tiny little cute kid with freckles but he would have done anything to protect me. My Dad didn't protect me from a lot worse than a couple of guys in an alley.

Unfortunately, that cute little freckled-faced boy was the first to give into the pressure he was receiving from my Dad.

He loved our Dad so much. When my Dad began calling him a coward and a sissy after he said no to the drugs, he caved in. He could not handle his Dad being mad at him and worse, making fun of him. My second brother who was a year younger followed not too far behind him.

Brothers

Within the year, the drugs began taking their toll. My brothers did not even look the same. Benny had a glazed, hardened look in his eyes now and did not seem to care about anything. My other brother became the same except, where Benny developed a mean streak like my Dad, he developed a very severe depression.

Benny started going out drinking with my Dad. I don't know how he got into the bars but he did. They would fight a lot when they were drinking and beat people up at the bar. My other brother started acting very scary. He started a fire in the shed that was in the back of our house and bragged about drowning some of our dog's puppies.

I tried to be as absent as possible. I would go to Church every service, go to my friend's house whenever possible and stay in my room reading when I was able.

Dad and my brothers would sit outside together and were always smoking pot. Benny started to act strangely and looked like a zombie. He had this scary blank stare and he wouldn't even respond to me when I talked to him. He would just stare right through me. I heard my Mom and Dad talking about it and they mentioned a drug called "angel dust". I think my Mom was worried but my Dad, of course, said it would be fine.

I asked my Mom about it and she told me a little about what it was. I just knew he was either going to die or commit a crime. After learning more about the drug, I was afraid he might even turn on one of us. I felt scared and helpless and sad that my brothers were in this situation and I hated my Dad for doing this to them.

39

My youngest brother, at the time, resisted the pressure from my Dad to join in with the drugs and because he resisted, he began to take the worst part of the verbal abuse. He was called every name my Dad could think of to shame him. One night, my Dad and Benny came home about 3:00 a.m. and I heard yelling. I froze as I always did, wondering what was going to happen and to whom.

My Dad pulled him out of bed and dragged him to the front yard. He told him to fight his brother and prove he was not a coward. He told him to toughen up. They started punching. It was a horrible thing to witness. Horrible. Yet he still went to school the next morning.

Despite the pressure from my Dad and brothers, my youngest brother still said no to the drugs and, in doing so, he endured name-calling, fights and my Dad's constant and favorite 'game' - putting out his foot to trip him as he walked by.

He went on to graduate High School and pursued a very successful professional career. Later, he would have a lot of tragedy in his life, including his fiancée being killed in a Los Angeles carjacking, drugs, prison and sadly dying of an overdose at the young age of 41.

My second brother went into his later teens joining a gang and got in far too deep. He lost a girlfriend to a serial killer, quit High School, was shot trying to protect my Mom from a gang member and served time in jail. He lost his wife (and love of his life) to a tragic accident resulting from a brain aneurysm. He is still an addict.

Martin was spared the drug pressure because of his disability.

After my Dad died, my eldest brother, my protector, my little freckled-faced friend, was unable to be ok without his partner in crime and he committed suicide not long afterward. He stood in the middle of a railway track and raised a beer to the oncoming train that killed him. It was 1985 and he had just turned 24 years old.

Sisters

My sisters seemed to be managing okay with all the craziness around them. They were all much younger than me and I believe that they have no memory of some of the stuff that went on in our home. I was still in charge of taking care of them a lot of the time and I think they looked at me as a mother figure.

I loved them so much. I wanted to take care of them and make sure they were never ever hurt or allowed to feel the pain that I had felt. My youngest sister became sick when she was 18 months old. As she had with my brother, my Mom rose to the challenge of a second child with special needs. She ferried my sister to all of the special schools and treatments.

One of my sisters left home before graduating High School and has not kept in contact with anyone. I wonder at times what she may have endured. By that time, I was out living on my own, far away from the childhood home that had been so horrific to me.

Chapter 5

"Go ye therefore, and teach all nations, baptizing them in the name of the Father, and of the Son, and of the Holy Spirit"

Matthew 28:19

Sex

My parent's sex life was used as a weapon in their arguments. I would wake up to my Dad ranting and raving about my Mom sleeping on the couch. There would be accusations of affairs and awful names would fly back and forth.

He did not respect women at all; they were objects to be leered at and used for sex. He used lewd language for every possible part of a woman's body. I never felt comfortable with my body as it developed from a child into a woman. I didn't want my breasts to develop and my Dad made sure to comment publicly when they did. I tried to ignore the feelings that my hormones were awakening inside of me. They felt dirty, shameful and I wanted no part of them. I wanted to remain a child and not become a woman - it felt wrong, bad and so disgusting.

To go to my bedroom or to leave the house, I had to walk by the dining table where my Mom and Dad sat, constantly chain-smoking. It became a terrifying journey for me. I can only remember a handful of times when I took that walk of shame and wasn't made fun of or leered at. It was where drug deals happened and it was where my Dad's "friends" would whistle, grab at me and make sexual comments at me.

When sex is made shameful to a child and adolescent, it makes growing into your body so confusing. When your hormones take control, an inner battle begins. On the one hand, you begin to feel a sexual awakening and, on the other, your mind is telling you it is wrong, dirty and disgusting to feel that way. It affects your intimacy toleration forever.

Church Molestation

Life continued the same at the Church. After one of the

services I attended, Brady, the boy who had molested me during the revival trip, came over and said that he was sorry about what had happened. He told me that he wanted to be friends and despite what had happened before, I was thrilled. I didn't care about what he had done anymore. I had the attention of this very good-looking boy and it made me feel good and wanted.

He said that I should talk to his sister about coming over to spend the night again so that we could see each other. I did and I was very excited when we were driving to their house after one of the services. He made sure he sat in the back with me. My friend rode in the front with her mother. As we drove, he reached his hand over and put it under my skirt and then my panties. He jammed his fingers into me as he had before and it hurt but I just sat there and let him. I did not want to ruin it this time and I definitely didn't want to be shunned again. I could see his mother's eyes in the rear-view mirror, and looking back on that day, I am pretty sure she knew what he was doing.

When we got to the house, he was so nice and gentle to me and I felt like things were going to be different this time. He told me to meet him in his room after everyone was asleep and I agreed. I was starting to feel nervous but I did not want to ruin this good feeling that I had inside. He really liked me.

When I went to his room, he told me to lie in bed with him to cuddle. I did and he put his arms around me. I felt the safest, most cared about that I had ever felt up to that moment. He said I should take my clothes off so we could be skin to skin. I definitely did not want to do that, but I found that the word "no" just wouldn't come out of my mouth. I was too scared to lose this feeling.

He scooted up behind me and put his arms around me. He then asked me to turn around and before I knew it, he had pushed me onto my back and straddled me. I was really scared now and told him that I didn't like this. He then told me to "shut up" and "not to make a sound" and then raped me violently. With every slap and every forceful thrust, I cried silent tears and told myself that I deserved it. I should have said no. When he put his penis in my mouth afterward, I somehow managed to hold back the vomit. I looked down at myself from above and was thoroughly disgusted by the girl that was me.

When he was done, he told me that if I told anyone, he would deny it and they would never believe me - just as they hadn't believed me before. I went back to bed in my friend's room and cried quietly all night long. I did not cry for the abuse, I was used to that. I didn't cry from the horrible physical pain that I felt, I was used to that. I cried because I had thought he really cared. I thought he really loved me for me. I cried because I had felt safe with a "man" for the first time in my life and it had been taken from me again.

The next morning, he acted as if nothing had happened. He went about his day and ignored me. He did not really want to be my boyfriend; he had got what he wanted. The pain of the abandonment was almost too much to bear. It was much worse than the physical pain. I didn't tell anyone about it this time. I had been through this with him before, and even though this was much worse, I was not going to go through that embarrassment again.

First Abortion

Things returned to the usual pattern of attending services, the abuse happening at home, school and staying with Kath whenever I could.

One morning, about a month later, I felt sick to my stomach. I was due to have my period, so I just figured it was going to be a bad one. It didn't come and I was terrified. I didn't want to tell anyone, but I finally told Kath about everything. She told me not to say anything because if I did, I would get into big trouble. She said she knew someone who would help me.

He was a friend of her family who also attended the Church and Kath said she would talk to him. He was 21 years old. He said he would help but that we mustn't tell anyone. He took me to a clinic where they made me pee in a cup. After a while, they came back and told me I was pregnant. How could I be pregnant? I was just a kid. She said there was no mistake.

The panic overwhelmed me and there was no way I could tell my Mom or anyone else in my family. He said he would take care of everything but that the members of the congregation could not know because of Brady being a respected member of the congregation.

That weekend, he brought me to a horrible place in a very scary part of Los Angeles. I went in and they had me fill out papers and he gave them some money. They took me into the back and put me on an examining table and then put my feet in stirrups. I was very scared now. The doctor told me it would only hurt for a minute and that he was "going to take the baby out of me". I started shaking. There was a horrible pain while the doctor did exactly that.

They gave me some relaxants afterwards and put me into a bed in another room. I fell asleep and when I woke up, there were about six other beds with drowsy women lying in them. No one was as young as I was and they were looking at me like I was from outer space. Then I remembered what had happened and I felt the most overwhelming sense of grief I had ever felt. I didn't want to be pregnant and I was not in a position to care for another human being, but I felt empty. Completely empty. I did not tell anyone about it ever. I never told my mother anything about it before she died. Brady had evidently been told because he came up to me at Church one day and said he was glad I got "rid of it" and to never tell anyone that it was his. I never did. Ever. Not until this minute.

There continued to be many embarrassing moments and many times where I felt unwanted, but the Church was my only outlet. The dress code continued to be especially difficult as I got into High School where I stood out from my peers. Always different.

Holy Ghost

There was a time during one of the Church services when everyone was standing up singing and I just started to cry. The words to the hymn were beautiful and I felt such a deep sadness for my life and a deep longing to go to this wonderful place that was talked about, a place where there was no sadness, no tears, only love and acceptance.

One of the women in the congregation came over to me and put her hand on my forehead and starting shouting "Praise God" and "Fill her with the Holy Ghost'. After a few minutes, there were congregation members gathered around me doing the same thing. I raised my hands as I was supposed to and started praying out loud "God save me."

I didn't feel any spirit entering me or anything but I did feel these people around me caring about me and wanting to save me from Hell. I kept praying and they kept praying and I got caught up in the excitement and started rambling gibberish. I did not feel any language from God coming through me but I wanted these people to be happy with me. I didn't want to disappoint them so I just spoke gibberish. They assumed I was receiving the Holy Ghost and as I had thought, they were very happy and pleased with me now that I was 'saved'.

A few weeks after my experience with the 'Holy Ghost', a baptism was set up and I was immersed, to be cleansed of all my sins. I felt like a liar and a cheat but I swallowed those feelings so I could experience the wonderful feelings of acceptance.

My family continued to make fun of me for attending the Church and for following all of their rules. I felt like an outcast and did not feel unconditional love anywhere. The love I received from the Church was conditional on me doing everything their way and being "good" and the love at home was always conditional upon some kind of favor, sexual or otherwise.

Exorcism

After the evening services, many of the families would go out together and have meals, snacks or gather at each other's houses. I was sometimes invited to these gatherings. In retrospect, I think that it was more a convenience for them to not have to drive me all the way home and then come back. Sometimes, they did do that but when I was invited, I felt so excited as it was such a treat for me.

One night, I was staying at one of the girl's homes for a sleepover and after Church, a few members of the congregation gathered at their house. This night wasn't the usual routine. There would usually be some snack food set out and the kids would play and the grown-ups would talk. This time, it felt much more serious. The adults were talking and the conversation was very hushed. I watched from the bedroom as one of the ladies sat down on the sofa and my friend's mother came in with a bowl of oil.

There were three people who began putting the oil on her forehead and she immediately began twitching and shouting out angrily. As this went on, the woman became more and more agitated and she began to hiss, curse and spit at the people around her and started shouting out in a foreign language (different from the speaking in tongues) and every time they put more oil on her, she screamed and writhed as if it hurt her.

My friend told me then that they were performing an exorcism! This so scared me. I was a constant reader of every kind of genre and I had read The Exorcist and knew that they had just made a movie out of it and that it was very controversial within the Churches. The Church we went to would never approve of this.

The things I had read in The Exorcist were terrifying to me and I could not believe this was happening right here in the house I was in. I thought that the demons she must possess would come alive just like they had in the book and enter us. We watched from the bedroom until we became tired and fell asleep. When we woke the next morning, the woman was gone and nothing was said to us but the adults were still talking in that hushed tone. Nothing was ever said about it after that and I didn't want to tell anybody because I was afraid they would think I was even crazier. I was utterly terrified of some evil spirit coming into my body.

Sleepover Nightmare

When I was in Junior High School, the Pastor's daughters surprised me by wanting to be my friend. I especially wanted to be friends with the youngest as she was the more popular one and peer acceptance was so important to me then.

She started talking to me and we hung out after Church services. She asked if she could come over for a sleepover. I said I would love for her to come and she said she would ask her Dad. I figured there was no way that he would let her come to my house knowing about my family, but she begged him and he finally said yes! I could not believe it! I was going to have the Pastor's daughter sleep over at my house. This was exceptional peer acceptance for me. Exceptional.

After the initial excitement, I remembered what she would be coming to. She lived in a beautiful house with a pool, up in the surrounding hills. I lived in a poor area with a shack for a house. You could not depend on my parents being sober and then there was the worst thing of all... cockroaches. We had had them in all of our houses in Los Angeles – they seemed to follow us everywhere. My Mom said it was impossible to get rid of them once you had them.

I told my Mom that the Pastor's daughter would be coming home with me after the Church service on Friday night. I told her that this was very important to me and asked if she and my Dad would please not drink that night. She said she knew how important it was and she promised me it would be fine. I reminded her again before I went to Church on Friday and she assured me it was going to be fine. I figured we could stay in my bedroom the whole time and I could try and hide the cockroaches by turning on the light before we walked in.

The worst happened. When we walked in, my parents were not there. The younger kids were there by themselves. I knew what that meant. They had gone to the bars to drink. This was not going to turn out well and I was frightened of what was to come. I had that familiar feeling as if I was watching this from above, these awful events happening below me. I took her into my room but in my panic, I forgot to turn the lights on first. I saw a few cockroaches run across the floor but I was pretty sure she hadn't seen them. Once the light was on, I knew I could watch for them.

I knew that my newfound friend could sense my tension when the front door slammed. I felt all white and frozen inside with the fear. My parents began their usual fighting, screaming, name-calling and cursing. The girl who I was so hoping to be friends with and accepted by asked to call her Dad because she wanted to go home.

It was a nightmare come real for me and I knew that was the last I would see of her. I didn't bother telling my Mom how much it had hurt and disappointed me. What good would it do? I just stuffed the anger, frustration, fear and confusion inside. I was getting good at doing that.

High School

I attended Verdugo High School during my Junior and Senior years even though I lived outside the catchment area. I was determined not to go to the school near us, which was in a rough area. I had attended there as a sophomore and had been scared every single day. One of the ladies at the Church allowed me to use her address so that I would qualify.

Verdugo High School felt safer to me. I wanted to coast through high school with no trouble and hopefully blend into the background. I loved it. I loved being able to choose some of my own classes and plan what I would do after high school. I loved having all the different subjects, which made school exciting for me.

I took typing and shorthand classes thinking that they

would get me a good job as a secretary. It came naturally to me and it filled me with a sense of pride and accomplishment. I was asked to participate in a national competition and though it frightened me, I was excited. We were to take dictation in shorthand and then transcribe it on a typewriter.

During the typing portion, my typewriter broke. They had to get me another one but it broke my concentration and my stride. When they were announcing the winners, to my great surprise, they called my name! I had come in second place! My school was very proud of me and my teacher felt I would have come in first place had my typewriter not broke. This fed my endless longing for approval and acceptance. Along with straight A's, teacher's comments and encouragement, I could not get enough.

I was still attending the Fundamentalist Church although I was backing off a bit. I would stop going for a while but then the nagging belief that I would go to Hell would drag me back. During the times when I wasn't going, I was called a backslider. We had been taught that anyone who left the Church was a backslider and would surely go to Hell.

During high school, I was starting to enjoy some independence from my family. I could take the bus on my own now and during my senior year, I started working at the Verdugo Adult School, which was located adjacent to the campus. Earning my own money was a wondrous feeling of freedom. We had been poor my entire life and with the job came my ticket out of that house, out of that nightmare and, most importantly, far away from my Dad.

I finished high school with a 4.0 grade point average and won a scholarship to college. My parents never knew about this or the competition I won.

Mormon

During my last year of high school, I met a very sweet girl who was in the same typing class as me. Her name was Whitney and she was Mormon. One day, while we were talking, I mentioned the Fundamentalist Church and told her about it. She was really supportive and started telling me about the Mormon Church.

She was not pushy at all and it sounded so different from what I had experienced and I agreed to go with her one day. The people were so different. They did not seem judgmental and they talked about a "Heavenly Father" who loved His children.

I wanted to believe this so desperately. I continued going and felt so loved. After a short while, I wanted to join this Church and be a part of it. That required another baptism. This time, though, my feeling of being accepted was genuine and the ceremony was gentle and spiritual, which was both new and wonderful to me.

In the Mormon community, I found that I was able to be myself more and more without fear of breaking rules or being condemned for not adopting the strict codes of a religion. I even allowed myself to be in a musical production with the teens! That was something I would never have done!

It was about the love and acceptance for me. My soul craved it. It felt as if I had a hole inside me and I never seemed to be able to fill it. What feelings of comfort I did absorb, I could not hold on to. They seemed to fade away or leak out when I was away from the situation that comforted me. I still fight that to this day – I struggle to retain feelings of self-worth, of acceptance or of love.

Whitney and I graduated high school together and then I got a full-time job and met my future husband. I lost touch with her soon after and stopped going to the Mormon Church. I did not feel judged by them for this but I did have that familiar voice inside telling me that I would surely go to Hell now that I had left two religions. I felt like a sinner and it confirmed my Dad's opinion that I did not belong.

Chapter 6

"Sometimes running away means you're headed in the exact right direction"

From the book 'Practical Magic' by Alice Hoffman

Leaving Home

❧

Ileft home when I was 17 years old. I had taken out a small Credit Union loan and bought my first car. It was an old beat up Datsun but it gave me freedom and I used those first wonderful moments to get out of there.

I gave my parents no warning. One Saturday, I went apartment hunting with a work friend, found a place the same day, came home and told my Mom that I would be moving out that same weekend. She was sad but not surprised. This was my escape and as much as I felt guilty that I was leaving her and my siblings alone with my Dad, I needed to be out of there. I would come back often to cook for my Mom and take the kids shopping with me but I vividly remember the feeling of relief – wanting to live my life and forget about all the years of horrors.

I had made it out, or so I thought. What I didn't realize at the time was that, although I had escaped from the physical presence of the abuse, it was still inside me, invisible but just as devastating. I couldn't escape the unhappiness that plagued me, the insecurities that kept me from taking chances and the craving for love and approval that always left me feeling unfulfilled and so, so lonely. It is indescribably sad to feel so lonely and only able to feel safe by being alone. I felt as if I was searching for something that would help the pain go away but I didn't quite know what that might be. It would be many years before I would come to a point where I would (or could) ask for help.

It is a very debilitating feeling when you need other people's love and approval to feel okay, but at the same time, you are so afraid of being hurt by their rejection that when anyone tries to give you that love and approval, you put up a wall and keep them as far away as possible. It leaves you constantly feeling empty inside.

Not until recently, in my fifties, was I able to open some of the

56

deepest pain and learn how my insecurities were simply my brain's way of dealing with the situation – the natural result of growing up in the crazy world that was my childhood. It is a wonderful feeling, now, to know that I can 're-learn' how to live and help the child inside me finally come to peace with the agonies of her past.

Chapter 7

"All happy families are alike; each unhappy family is unhappy in its own way."

Anna Karenina by Leo Tolstoy, 1873

Jack

I met my future husband at work, very soon after moving out on my own in 1977. Jack was the first man that I had an interest in who, when he returned the interest, didn't make me run away. In fact, I clung to him for dear life! It was a foreign feeling for me. I felt like I was a virgin when I met him even though, technically, monsters had stolen that part of me. It was as if all my sexual feelings came out with him and most of them felt okay.

I immersed myself in him. I developed an extreme dependence on him for my happiness. While we were dating, he was my sole reason for waking up each morning. I neglected my friends and cut off all other interests in my life, barely leaving the phone for fear I might miss a call from him. We had a consistent sexual relationship but there were certain aspects of sex that I "suffered" through. I had no idea how to say no to anything, even some things that filled me with fear.

Birth control was something I would never have talked to my mother about. It was also something that I was too shy and fearful to mention to Jack. He made it clear that he did not want to be "tied down" in a relationship and that triggered my insecurity, made my fears worse and made me withdraw further from 'difficult' conversations.

So, not surprisingly, within two months of dating, I found out I was pregnant again. I knew that I hadn't used any birth control, but I guess I just didn't think it would happen again. There was no question as to what should happen, and Jack made an appointment for me to have the abortion. It was pretty much the same experience as before but the sadness, the emptiness and the loneliness were even worse. This time, the baby came from what felt like love.

I never told Jack about the previous abortion or any details of the sexual abuse I had endured. I distanced myself from that and tried to create a new life. I told him nothing of my family and how poor we were. I never told him exactly where I lived and would just give him a general area. When I first met his parents, they knew nothing of my background. I created another lie, another false existence to distance myself from the madness and an attempt to be "normal".

Pot

Jack first found out part of my real life when he had bought some marijuana from a friend who had bought it from my Dad! When he confronted me about it, I tried to deny it and talk my way around it but I think he knew I was lying. Jack smoked pot regularly with his friends and despite all of the opportunities, I had never tried that, or anything. Not ever. Not even a cigarette. Smoking, drinking and using drugs were things that meant death to me. It meant being like my Dad and I NEVER wanted that to happen. I had not said goodbye to him when I left home and I never spoke to him again. After pressure from Jack, I tried smoking pot with him one evening but I had a wild hallucination and never did it again. There is a part of me deep inside that still feels guilty for that and that I failed myself.

We had been dating for about two years and, during that time, we had many problems mainly arising from me smothering Jack with my clinginess and my insecurities. I now understand that I was completely codependent upon Jack, but at the time, I always felt as if he were about to leave me and he would never commit to anything, even telling me I was on "trial". I was depressed, irritable and ill at ease constantly during that time. We did have fun together going places and doing things but the tension was slowly increasing.

Northern California

In 1979, Jack decided to move to Sonoma County after his family made plans to live there. His older brother had been married a couple of years earlier and had moved there to start a family and to be nearer his wife's parents. I felt like my world had ended. I had no one.

I became anorexic for a while. I barely ate, ran every chance I could get and became skeletal, yet still believed I was fat and ugly. In early 1980, with no promise of even being Jack's "girlfriend", I decided to follow him, get my own apartment and get a new job there. I packed my things up, rented a U-Haul trailer and moved. I was very sad to leave my Mom and siblings but that spark of hope inside me had never left and it gave me the courage to do anything I could to be loved.

Soon after I arrived in Northern California, Jack and I moved in together, still with no commitment of anything. After 2 more years of being together, I asked him if we should just get married. He did not propose to me, he just agreed.

When his mother found out that we planned to marry, she was livid about it and spent a lot of time and effort trying to convince him it was a mistake. When I first met her, she seemed to like me, but as time went on, she had started to think I was not good enough for him.

What his mother thought of me was, however, the least of my worries. After we got engaged, there was no avoiding the inevitable. Jack was finally going to have to meet my family.

Families

We drove down to Los Angeles where my family still lived and I spent the whole journey paralyzed with fear and anxiety. I was sure that once Jack saw what it was like there and where I had come from, he would leave me. I had still given him no idea of my "other" life. I prayed that the visit would be ok and I had no idea how I would handle things if things were as bad as they could be.

When we arrived, I could barely breathe and I was on the verge of a full panic attack. My Mom and my brother came out to the car when we pulled up. They say that people who live with addicts and abusers become incredibly attuned to their moods and as soon as I saw them, I knew that things were as bad as they could be. My Mom was staggering, which meant she was drunk. My brother was high as usual and God knows what shape my Dad would be in (and I hadn't talked to him since I moved out). What a nightmare. I was never going to get away from being that dirty little girl who was worthless.

It was a truly hellish weekend. The second we walked into the house, I wanted to be back in our little apartment in Sonoma County. Jack was in shock at everything he saw. I had told him that we didn't have a lot of money and that my Dad and I didn't really get along but he was completely unprepared for the reality and the extent of the dysfunction and poverty.

Everybody drunk, high on drugs, chain-smoking – and the cockroaches still out in force – it all made me wish that a hole would open up so I could sink deep into it.

Driving home, Jack did ask a few questions but we really didn't talk about it at any length. I sat in silence, frozen by the feelings that had been brought up by the awful visit. I knew that Jack would be telling his parents. Why did it always follow me?

Things were different almost immediately when we got back to Sonoma County. Jack's family, especially his mother and brother, treated me differently than they had before. They ignored me, made nasty comments and treated me as if I was 'not good enough' to be in their family. Jack and I started arguing more and more. I would be hurt by the way they would treat me and his response was to defend them – telling me that I was imagining it and that they were not treating me as I knew they were. I felt betrayed by him because he would never stand up for me to them.

We had also begun to have sexual difficulties and this was before we had even got married! Although I was still able to function, I just didn't enjoy it like I used to. I started to feel that if he loved me enough to have sex with me, he should stand up for me to his family when they attacked me.

It was a very difficult time for me. I can still remember gritting my teeth through the whole sex thing waiting for it to finally be over and when, thankfully, it was, I would turn over and cry. It was very lonely but I never let him know what I was feeling. My recent work on my stored trauma has taught me that I was using the same protection with Jack that I had used during the earlier abuse. I had honed the skill of dissociation and was able to put myself in a place where no-one could reach me and where I was apart from what was happening to my body.

A funeral

Over the coming weeks, we were planning our wedding but I was not enjoying the process as most young brides seem to. I was filled with anxiety and a deep sense of loathing. My family would be there and I just never knew what to expect or what would happen. There was no way that I wanted my father walking me down the aisle. Jack's mother and brother became more and more sarcastic with me and seemed to delight in bringing up the subject as if they knew it made me uncomfortable. I started to wish my Dad was dead. I felt so guilty at feeling that. The thought would come into my head but I would try and force it out because it made me feel like an awful person.

Our wedding was set for April 1982 and one evening in mid-December, Jack came home and told me that my Dad had died. He was 44 years old and had committed suicide. I thought Jack was joking (not that it would have been particularly amusing) and I didn't believe him right away. Do you know what my first thought was? It was that I would definitely now go to Hell and there was no way around it. I had not done everything I could to get my Dad converted to the Fundamentalist Church and now it was too late.

The depth of the damage that Church did to me still lives with me today. I have seen testimonials by other people who attended the same *Fundamentalist Church around the same time and their experience was eerily similar to mine. The fact that people can instill such deep anxiety and fear in children is bad enough but to do so in the name of a loving God is beyond my comprehension. I am working hard to heal from the damage they did but it is hard not to believe that I am destined for eternal damnation for things I have done.*

We went to the funeral and the Church was packed. There was standing room only at the back of the chapel. It was an open casket and it scared me to see him lying there. I felt like I shouldn't be there. There were so many people, most of them young people my brother's age that he had dealt drugs to. I had no feelings of sadness. I was numb. I remembered how I had wanted to be loved by him and have a Dad who took care of me. I felt sad that I couldn't feel sad.

As we were walking past the casket, I stopped, looked at him and he looked strange but not scary anymore. I leaned down to kiss him, wanting to say goodbye and feel something, anything, but I didn't. I just felt like the fool he always thought I was.

A wedding

We had our wedding even though Jack's mother was trying to stop him. He told me sometime later that she had taken him aside right before the ceremony and begged him not to marry me. My family came and stayed with Jack's family, which I knew would be a disaster. The reception was at Jack's parents' house as well and we did have a really good time. After we got back from our honeymoon, we found out that my family had got drunk, made a big mess and my Mom was so embarrassed that she got them up and left in the middle of the night without saying goodbye.

Several months after our wedding, I found out I was pregnant. I was ecstatic. I felt thrilled. It seemed worth enduring sex to have this life growing inside of me. I felt like things were finally going to have meaning. I was wrong.

When I was 11 weeks pregnant, almost past the danger zone, I had a miscarriage. It devastated me. Jack had not been thrilled initially by the pregnancy but after the miscarriage, he realized how much he had wanted the baby. I believed it was punishment for having the abortions.

We wanted to become pregnant again immediately and, all of a sudden, sex was okay again. There was a purpose to having sex and it was the creation of life. It didn't take long before I was pregnant again and this time we were both ecstatic.

A daughter

After I knew I was pregnant, our sex life went downhill again. I felt used again and it seemed that if there was no purpose to have sex, that it was wrong, dirty and shameful. I slowly pulled away from him again until sex was completely off limits. I used my pregnancy and every other excuse I could think of to avoid it.

After our daughter was born in 1984, I felt completely fulfilled as a mother and as a person. I never knew it was possible to love someone so much. It totally consumed me. I was determined from the start of her life that she would never suffer the way I had suffered as a child.

I was and still am very protective of my children. There have been times when I have had to force myself to let them experience things on their own without trying to make sure nothing bad or humiliating happens to them. I felt and still feel their pain to an inappropriate extent. I am extremely sensitive to them being disciplined in front of people because of the way I was constantly criticized and humiliated in public.

After her birth, I constantly used excuses (such as exhaustion) to avoid sex. I began to feel very uncomfortable if I was even alone with my husband for any length of time. She was never a good sleeper – from the moment we brought her home, she fought naps and bedtime. She would be happy while she was awake but she just didn't want to sleep.

We tried everything. When she was about 8 months old, I convinced Jack to let her sleep in our bed with us. We weren't getting sleep and we were beginning to argue in the middle of the night about what to do with her. It seemed a perfect solution to me. We could both get a good night sleep and I could avoid sex.

We began to argue a lot about our sexual problem. He would lose his patience and make me promise to go and see a therapist and I would convince him that I could work it out on my own. I couldn't imagine ever talking to a stranger about this problem. The longer I was able to avoid sex, the harder it became to even think about it. I began to find excuse after excuse to avoid being alone with him.

I always made sure our daughter was with us or I would wait until he went to bed, and after he was asleep, I would sneak into bed under the covers. It became such a fear to me that it began consuming a major portion of my days, planning to avoid being alone with him. I began to make excuses not to go out to dinner or go to a movie with him. The risk of being alone or being touched was too great.

Needless to say, this was a very rocky period in our marriage. I honestly don't know how we survived it as long as we did. There were many arguments, many bitter words and broken promises and the constant tension, day in and day out, was becoming unbearable.

A Son

The next major hurdle for me sexually was when I wanted to have another baby. I wanted two children, spaced two to three years apart. Having grown up with seven brothers and sisters, I didn't want our daughter to be an only child. When she was two, I began thinking of a plan for me to become pregnant. I was petrified of sex. We had not been together since the end of my pregnancy! It was quite a dilemma. Not only had we not had sex in almost two years, we had not been alone more than once or twice that whole time.

A month after our daughter's second birthday, I

calculated the optimum day in my cycle and it was one of the scariest days of my life. I felt as if I would die - it was awful. I remember crying afterwards feeling as if there was something terribly wrong with me. Was I crazy? No matter how hard I tried, I just couldn't shake the feelings of shame and disgust. Sometimes I would wonder if I had fallen out of love with him, but when I thought of life without him, it was unbearable. It was so confusing. I just wanted to feel normal. I used to wish that Jack and I could just be friends – I felt that would be a perfect way to live but, of course, he would never be satisfied with that.

Much to my relief, I did not have to go through it again - our one episode resulted in a pregnancy, much to his disappointment.

I had a very rough pregnancy with my son. From the very beginning, I had severe morning sickness and in my second trimester, I contracted a bad strain of flu, which developed into pneumonia and I ended up in hospital. I was very weak through the whole pregnancy. The only blessing of being so sick was that it gave me a valid reason to avoid intimacy with my husband. I always felt safe if there were good excuses to avoid it. If there weren't good excuses, I felt guilty and crazy.

Our son, Jason, was as wonderful a gift as our daughter had been. Once again, I was consumed by a feeling of fulfillment. My children showed me that I could love and be loved unconditionally - something I had never before understood.

With two children to provide me with reasons to avoid intimacy with Jack, our relationship continued in the same way that it always had. We would get along okay for a while, then the tension would begin mounting and there would be the inevitable argument with him saying he couldn't live a celibate life and me promising I could work it out on my own. Sometimes, I felt as if I could work it out but I was never able to – the deep fear of sex always won in the end.

Jack started to insist that I see a therapist. I kept saying I would call someone and I did see that it was probably the best thing to do but when it would come to making the call,

I just couldn't. I was much too frightened to talk about my 'problem' with a stranger.

By the time our daughter turned 3 years old, she was still sleeping in our bed. Jack would insist that it was time we get her used to her own bed. I made some half-hearted attempts but she always ended back between us. I only felt safe when she was there. The horrible shame and fear were still stealing my happiness and my peace. The horror of my childhood followed me everywhere no matter how far I tried to run from it.

Outwardly, we functioned as a good family. We went on family outings but Jack and I never went anywhere as husband and wife. We would have fun doing things with the kids but I always sensed his desire to be alone with me and that brought up a turmoil of emotions in me; I felt afraid, guilty and inadequate at the same time. We lived like this for several years. They were not all bad years but were a repeating cycle of tension and broken promises.

Chapter 8

"In this sad world of ours sorrow comes to all and it often comes with bitter agony."

Letter to Fanny McCullough, Abraham Lincoln, 1862

Mom

In March of 1992, at the age of 50, my Mom died after a short illness. She was a chain smoker and the emphysema took its toll on her lungs. I am sure the alcohol and lifestyle contributed too. It was totally devastating to me. I depended on her for everything. I called her almost every day. If Jack and I had a fight, she was the one I had called. If I got depressed, she was the one I had called. She had become my life force and she felt like the only person in the world who accepted me for who I was. My husband had once said to me he worried about what would happen to me if she died, as she seemed to hold me together. He was right.

For many years, I believed that my Mom's death was my 'low point', that I had 'hit rock bottom'. I now realize that it was not. The agony of losing my Mom was one pain too much and the walls that I had built to hold in the results of my horrific experiences could no longer keep back the pent-up emotions. Unfortunately, this led to a very low period of my life as I battled the ensuing depression. Recently, I have been taught that the trauma I suffered got 'stored' within my brain and would continue to dictate my reactions and leave me yearning for the attention and validation that I did not get as a child. My Mom's passing was a turning point in my life. It started me on the road to recovery, but at the time, it felt as if my world had come to an end.

Part One Footnote

Losing my Mom was more than losing a parent – I lost the only person who I felt I could talk to about how I was feeling. I had never talked to her about what my Dad had done but I had shared what was happening with Jack and to lose my only confidant was especially painful. Although I now realize that I had a very codependent relationship with my Mom (evolved from my earliest childhood when I felt responsible for looking after her or managing the kids when she couldn't), we did grow to share a very strong bond and I felt that losing her was like losing part of me.

Over the coming months, I wrote letters to my Mom as a way to 'keep in touch' and to keep the bond alive. Reading these now, I can still feel the powerful emotions and the deep sadness and helplessness that I felt.

August 21, 1992
Dear Mom,

I really need to talk to you so I'm going to write to you. I wish so bad I could see you and talk to you about all that's happening. A lot has happened since you've been gone. I think you'd be proud of me and what I'm trying to do. I've been dealing with a lot of things to do with Dad that in some ways I wish I could talk to you about and in some ways it might be best if I didn't. I would never want to hurt you. I love you so much and truly know in my heart that you were a victim of Dad as I was. I really hate him for what he did to me and is still causing me to go through. I realize things were tough on him but he hurt me so bad, down to my soul. I'm trying to get over it but sometimes it feels like an uphill battle. Just when I think I can make it to the top I start falling again. We just found out Jeni has diabetes. Boy I could really use to talk with you about that. I wish you were here to talk to Jeni. I know you could make *her feel better. You always could. She is scared and feeling different and alone. I want her to be okay. I love you so so much.*

There's just so much going on and I'm trying to be strong but sometimes I feel so alone. No matter what Jack says nobody can really understand me like you did. I don't think it's possible unless you live under our roof and the type of home that we all lived in. I miss that no matter what happens or how hard things are. God I could always count on you to love me with all my faults. I'm trying to fix some of those faults like not trusting people. Trust is very hard for me. You are the only one I ever totally trusted. I hope you're happy wherever you are. Sometimes I feel bad because I don't think of you all the time but sometimes it's easier not to deal with it so it doesn't hurt. I'm so tired of hurting like I do.

I feel waves of depression over me now and I feel like I'm drowning in it. I wish I could drown. I hope you know how much I wanted to make you better. I really felt I could help you get better. I never thought you would not make it. If I had only known I would've come down a lot sooner and maybe I could have got you treatment sooner. I would have stayed and held your hand that morning and been with you when you left this world. I wonder where you are.

December 1992
Dear Mom

I wish so bad I could talk to you. I miss you and sometimes can't believe you're not here to care about me and to listen to me. I always felt like you gave me hugs on the phone and boy do I need a hug from you. Jack wants to comfort me and give me hugs and even though I know that's all he would do I just can't seem to feel better.

I hope you understand why I'm doing what I'm doing. I know you would never have hurt me intentionally or purposely. I think Daddy loved me in his own way. I'm trying to get through all this so I can have my life back. I want to feel happy. I never quite make it. I love you so much. I know if you could have given us a different life you would have. I wish I could just leave it behind. I hope you're not mad at me.

I hope you believe all the things that he did to me. Sometimes I have a hard time believing he did this to me. I hope you're happy where you are. You deserve peace. It seems like there's this place in me that you filled and I can't fill that hole. But I'm trying.

You always encouraged me to get help and try to work things out with Jack. I hope you are proud of me. Jeni misses you so much. Sometimes I don't know what to tell her. I feel so out of control right now. I can't even get through the day without falling apart. I want what I can't seem to ever get. Someone to love me and be proud of me like you were unconditionally.

I'm sorry I just can't seem to feel anything but hate for Dad. He hurt me so bad. I feel he made me weak like him. Sometimes I feel strong and sometimes I just feel I want to be away from everything. I don't want to die but I don't want to feel this way. Nobody understands how much it hurts.

I took some pills and they made it go away but only for a while. Then it got worse. It scared me because I've never done anything like that before. Lately I feel I want to take a few extra to numb the pain. How can I ever make it on my own? I always need somebody. I have two great kids. I love them so much and I wouldn't want to leave them. But I hate that they see me like this. Will

I ever be able to cope on my own? I found a really good doctor. He seems to really care but he is a doctor and not a father and one day I won't have him. He's the only one beside you I've ever been able to trust and who seems to understand me or who cares to understand me. I wonder if everyone would be better off without me and my problems.

Part Two:
Don't Expect Me To Lie

Chapter 9
"All the king's horses and all the king's men couldn't put Humpty together again"
Humpty Dumpty (English nursery rhyme), 18th Century

Therapy

My Mom's death was to be the catalyst for me to finally seek help. The only thing that got me up each day was the fact that I needed to take care of my kids. I was always able to pull myself together in the end for them. I loved them more than life and fought very hard for them to have a secure and loving home. They had always been able to come to me about anything that was bothering them (and they still can). I had never had a secure home environment where I could feel safe and I desperately wanted that for them.

Two weeks after my Mom died was our 11th wedding anniversary. Our anniversary was always a very difficult day for me because there were expectations of me that I could not fulfill. I thought that this particular year would be tolerable because my Mom had just died and I thought that Jack would be sympathetic to my feelings of loss. I was mistaken. The night of our anniversary, I slept with the kids on our sofa bed. They liked to do that once in a while; it was like camping out in the family room. Shortly after my husband had gone to bed, he got up and slammed out of the house. I was shaking inside and out because I knew I had crossed another line with his patience. The following day was tense silence. I was angry that he would push me at a time when I was in such deep mourning over the loss of my Mom.

After a few days of silence, the tension finally blew up. Jack told me he could not live like this anymore. By this time, it had been 7 years of sexless marriage. I promised again that I would find a therapist and he said that if I didn't, things were over. Those words rang over and over in my ears for the next few days and I knew that if I did not make an effort to find out what was wrong with me, I would lose him forever and I could not bear another loss so soon after my Mom's death. I felt totally hopeless, depressed and confused. It was a turning point in my life and looking back, I am glad that he gave me that ultimatum, as it forced me to get help.

I began the task of finding a therapist. It took me a couple of weeks and it was one of the hardest things I had ever done in my life. I wanted to be as sure as I could before I went to see someone that I would feel comfortable enough to be able to talk. I called several doctors and each call was terrifying. Each time, I would have to explain a little about my 'problem'. I presented it to them as depression over my Mom's death and not being able to be 'close' to people.

It was very difficult. My emotions were raw. I could tell by talking to some of them that I would not feel comfortable for various reasons. I finally found a psychiatrist who seemed kind on the phone and someone I thought I might be able to talk to.

After making the appointment, I was a nervous wreck! I thought of a million reasons why I should cancel the appointment. I began to think a psychiatrist would laugh me out of his office and tell me my problems were not serious enough. I was especially worried about that. Growing up, I always felt like I was going crazy and needed to talk to someone but no one ever seemed to care or think my problems were serious enough or worth listening to.

I don't even remember getting to his office for the first visit. I was sure I would never make it. I now know that it was a very courageous step. Admitting that I needed help was the beginning of the end of the secrecy and silence, which had been so destructive to my life. It was also the beginning of my transformation from a victim to a survivor. Everyone who has suffered from sexual abuse and its devastation deserves to feel that strength and the hope to overcome its effects on life and self-esteem. We deserve to be happy again.

Dr. Graham

Fortunately, my efforts to find a good therapist paid off. I knew from the first visit that this was someone who would understand what I was going through. It was a relief to have someone prepared to listen to my attempts at explaining what I felt my problems were and to be able to summarize my life in a way I had never been able to. It was as if he could see how I felt inside, without me having to explain. All my life, I had felt that no one understood how much pain I had inside me and, even worse, that no one cared about that pain. I remember clearly the look on his face when he asked me about our sex life and I told him it had been non-existent for 7 years. I couldn't believe I had actually admitted that huge secret to someone.

He raised his eyebrows at that admission, but somehow didn't make me feel like I was an alien from outer space. I was very depressed about my Mom's death and feeling very hopeless. At the end of that first visit, I clearly remember him telling me that although he knew I felt hopeless, he saw hope for me and he felt I had a good chance to work things out.

I left feeling so relieved. It was such a good feeling to have someone tell me there was hope! It was the first time ever in my life that there was even a glimmer on the horizon. Someone actually thought my problems were worth listening to! It is actually very sad to realize that I had never before felt that sense of self-worth. I was beaten down so much emotionally that I had never experienced the feeling that comes when someone really listens to you and cares about what you have to say. My Mom had listened to me but it wasn't the same. She didn't really know how to give me hope.

For the time between that first visit and my next, I was very happy. I was scared about opening up to someone but I felt so relieved that I had found a therapist I liked and who seemed to care and who, most amazingly, didn't think I was crazy! My husband was also happy that I had finally made the first step and that gave me confidence.

Well, it got much harder fast! During my next couple of sessions, he probed into areas I thought were buried safely away inside me. There were so many things about my past that I had made myself forget that came bubbling up to the surface.

It was the beginning of an emotional roller coaster that both Dr. Graham and I were powerless against. I would leave his office and my mind would be flooded with memories and flashbacks of my past abuse. It was so difficult to dig it all up because, for so many years, I had compartmentalized my past and kept it safely locked away where it 'belonged'. To start letting it out even little by little was absolutely terrifying and very painful.

Over the next few months, many more memories would become crystal clear. It was as if each time my therapist validated my feelings and memories, it made me feel a little safer and it allowed something else to come out. During this early therapy, I became extremely depressed and constantly felt overwhelmed with the extent of the emotions. I couldn't sleep, I was losing weight and barely functioned from day to day. He raised the possibility of medication during my 2nd or 3rd visit and suggested that I start taking Prozac.

A particular incident that had happened when I was an adolescent kept coming up in my mind. Over and over. I will never forget how difficult it was for me to tell my therapist about it. It took almost the whole hour to even begin and I remember sitting in that chair trying to speak the words and just not being able to get them out. I squirmed uncomfortably wanting to sink into the chair and be anywhere else in the world than in that office. I would start with a few words and then not be able to continue.

I think after a while, he probably had a good idea of what I was on the verge of saying but he wouldn't say it for me. I wished more than anything that he would just say the words and I could just say, "Yes, that is what happened". He encouraged me to continue and told me that if it was making me this uncomfortable to even say the words aloud, imagine what it had been doing to me on the inside all of these years. He told me it was like poison eating away at me and I needed to let it out before it continued to harm me. It still took every ounce of willpower in me to say the words.

Finally, I managed to tell him about one New Year's Eve when we went to one of my Dad's friend's house. I was watching TV and the man had come and sat and put his arm around me. He started moving his arm closer and closer to my breasts, touching me. There was no one else in the room and I was praying inside someone would come in. No one came in to check. My parents and their friends were in that house. How was this able to happen to me without anyone knowing? Again, not only did my Dad think he could molest me, but he cared so little of me that he let his friends use me too.

The feelings of shame that I felt after this particular therapy session were very strong. I was very emotional and felt completely drained – like being run over by a truck. It was the beginning of my journey through an unbelievable amount of pain that was to come through recalling some pretty awful things. It was also the beginning of my journey out of the 'black hole' and into a delicate light of hope.

Dr. Graham warned me that now I was talking about the abuse, buried memories were beginning to push their way out of their hiding places and that I may be overwhelmed with graphic images at any time or place. He wanted me to understand this so that I would not think I was losing my mind when it occurred. I would go home and these thoughts, feelings and images would envelop me. They would put me into a depression for a few days and then I would feel okay for a few days and then it would be time to go back and dredge up more poison.

Dreams

I had been on Prozac for a few weeks now and there were signs that it was helping. I was able to sleep and had more energy. However, I also began having some pretty detailed dreams.

Over the next couple of months, things became more and more difficult; I had no control over the images that would flash in my mind at times. I felt as if I wanted to stop the whole process but was powerless to do so. I started having headaches, nausea, nightmares and insomnia. I was always on the verge of tears and constantly irritable with my family.

I also felt a lot of denial. I felt as if I really was crazy to be having all these vivid flashbacks. I knew that I had been sexually abused but, for so long, I had locked the details away in my mind. Now it was as if the walls I had built to keep them in were crumbling and I was powerless to stop these images. I felt as if I was reliving all of it. I wanted so badly to go back to when I remembered only what I chose to remember.

At this time, I was having nightmares every night, some recurring night after night. One particularly frightening one that recurred was of being in my house and knowing that someone is outside waiting for the right moment to break in. In my dream, I was petrified and scared for my life. Another was of being in a public place, realizing I didn't have any clothes on or trying to go to the bathroom and not finding one that was not open to public view. Looking back, these recurring nightmares were most often filled with a feeling of being exposed and powerless to avoid it.

In one dream that I still have from time to time, I am driving a Volkswagen Bug up an extremely steep hill and I keep having to shift gears down to keep moving. I never quite make it to the top and the car starts slipping downhill, so I get out and walk over the top of the hill. I am very dirty and sweaty and come across a shower, so I go in, take off my clothes and start to wash. There is no door on the shower and a lady with blonde hair comes up to the open door with a knife in her hand which she holds up as if to stab me. Then I wake up.

I would go see my therapist and be unable to talk about the images that were flooding my mind. I would 'zone out' and wish I could disappear. He would push me, knowing that I needed to let it out but I would keep it inside.

For a few days after a session, I would wish that I could talk to him and tell him everything. I wanted so badly for someone to care about what I had to say but as soon as I would get to his office the next week, I would withdraw again. I wished for courage and, at the same time, wanted to run away as fast as I could until I was far, far away from any of it.

If I kept busy, it was easier for me to clear my mind but as soon as I had any quiet time, I was helpless. For reasons I did not understand, my emotions would especially overwhelm me in the shower. I don't know if it was because I was alone with no interruptions, but the pictures always began to come when I was in the shower. I would find myself scrubbing myself raw without even realizing it. I would feel sick to my stomach and unable to stop crying.

This went on for a while before I was able to tell Dr. Graham the details. He gave me tremendous support and encouragement but it just felt so shameful to me. I didn't want him to think badly of me. I felt that if anyone knew what was going through my mind, they would be shocked and disgusted.

The secrecy and stigma that accompanies the crime of sexual abuse is so prominent and so deep in our minds that it is almost impossible to ever tell anyone. We are told that no one will believe us, people will be mad at us; they will think we are damaged and dirty. Those feelings were so much a part of me that it was very difficult to tell even when I was safe and with someone who only wanted to help me.

However, it is crucial to get it out in the open if we are ever to recover. The secrecy must be destroyed and you need to have your story listened to by someone who will react to you with compassion and understanding. Someone who will help you understand that it wasn't your fault, you were a victim of a very sick person(s) and you must fight to not let that person(s) destroy the survivor in you. I was lucky to have such a person; I was slowly able to reach a point where I was able to tell him some of my secrets.

Deeper memories

I was floating on a lounger in our pool one weekend. My therapist and I had been working on ways for me to become comfortable being alone with my husband. He had explained to me that every time I 'tolerated' any closeness it was as if I was reliving my abuse. He encouraged me to experiment with taking the initiative in order to show myself that I could be in control. So, this day, I asked Jack if he wanted to lay on the double lounger with me. This may seem like a small thing to most people but to me, it was a very scary thing to lay that close to him.

I had still not been alone with him for years. He seemed surprised that I had offered but, thankfully, didn't make a big deal out of it. He got on the lounger with me and I scooted to the very edge of my side so as not to have to touch him. I did a pretty good job, but not good enough. My arm was at my side with his right next to it. I succeeded in not touching his skin but I could feel the hairs of his arm touching my arm. My eyes were closed and, all of a sudden, in my mind it wasn't my husband lying next to me, it was my Dad. I felt as if it was my Dad's arm and I could see his face clearly. It was very frightening. I opened my eyes and jerked my arm away.

I told Dr. Graham about it at my next session. A long time afterwards, he told me that he had suspected that this vivid image was a precursor to what I was to remember next.

In the next few sessions, I was finally able to tell him about some of the images I saw constantly in my mind. They were crystal clear and they were horrible. It was what I now think of as the first really bad memory of the sexual abuse that I was able to say out loud.

The words did not just flow easily out of my mouth – it was the most difficult thing I had experienced since I began therapy. I had come to a point where I just had to get it out. It was like an infection that had festered for a long time and would never heal until the poison was out. The emotions that came with it, however, were almost unbearable.

Finally, I described the incident he had known was coming. I described it as I remembered it – as if it were happening again and I was reliving every painful aspect of it. It was the memory of being molested by my Dad at 4 years old. I could see the room clearly, my blanket (with the soft part on top), the curtains in the window and the door open a crack with the hall light streaming in. I felt very scared. My Dad was standing over me. I didn't see his face, but I feel him standing there. I'm pretending to be asleep. I feel his face between my legs. I feel his stubble. His tongue. I then feel his penis in my mouth. The hair. The wrinkled flesh of his testicles. The smell of alcohol. I look down from above and wish I could destroy him.

Over the years, the tension of wondering if this would be 'one of the nights' my Dad entered my room was debilitating. I would listen for every sound and every footstep, scared to death. Some nights I would fall asleep while waiting. Other nights he would come in and I would go away in my mind.

I cannot describe what it was like to share this memory with my therapist, except that it was as if I relived every single moment and felt the fear, disgust and emotions as clearly as if it was all happening again. It was very difficult to tell him – he wouldn't fill in any of the pauses, even though I'm positive he had a good idea of what was coming. I had to be the one to finally tell the ugly secrets that had been buried for so long, working their poison inside of me.

To my great surprise, Dr. Graham reacted with genuine concern. Shockingly and opposite to what I assumed would happen, he didn't seem to look at me any differently. Was it possible that I wasn't really disgusting and that people might still like me? There were so many emotions I felt when I let this memory out. I felt exhausted – it had taken all my strength and courage to get it out. I felt so sad because, somehow, telling it to someone made it more real – now I couldn't file it away again and pretend it hadn't happened. However, I also felt relieved and felt another glimmer of hope. I had told someone about a secret without being blamed. More importantly, what I shared had been believed – the opposite of what I had been told, as a child, would happen.

Childhood Sexual Abuse and incest are crimes of secrecy. Dr. Graham explained that each time I told him about something that had happened to me and my sharing wasn't met with disgust, it would be another step towards healing.

Chapter 10

"Our wounds are often the openings into the best and most beautiful part of us."

David Richo

Dependence

Well, I felt pretty good for a while after sharing one of the most painful memories but it wasn't long before more poison needed to be let out. It seemed as if whenever I would let something out, there was something else waiting to surface. It was as if my mind would only let me remember so much at one time.

Dr. Graham explained that your mind does protect you against what it can't handle. He explained to me that Post Traumatic Stress Disorder is a mental health condition that's triggered by a terrifying event(s) – either experiencing it or witnessing it. Symptoms may include flashbacks, nightmares and severe anxiety, as well as uncontrollable thoughts about the event. Sometimes I desperately wanted to go back to before I started talking about this stuff. It hurt far too much. But I also didn't want it to ruin my life, so most of the time, I just felt as if I was stuck.

Looking back, it was around this time that I really began to realize how much I had longed for a Dad who cared about me. I had unconsciously been looking for that my whole life. I began to feel those fatherly feelings towards my therapist. Dr. Graham was about the same age as my Dad would have been if he had lived and he really seemed to care about me. Part of the power of therapy (but also one of the potential pitfalls) is the transferring of your parental feelings onto your therapist. I had begun to feel as if I could never imagine being without him there to talk to and to listen to me and to show me compassion and validation of my feelings. He really understood when no one had ever cared enough to try.

I began to wish he were my Dad even though I knew he couldn't be. I brushed it off and tried not to let him see that I felt so strongly about it – I didn't want him to see the depth of the dependency I was fostering. I also figured that it must be normal to feel that way – I knew that part of a good therapeutic relationship was having a therapist who genuinely cared; someone I genuinely trusted. I just knew I would never be able to not have him there for me. This dependency kept growing and started to turn into a very intense fear that, if I ever did anything wrong, he would leave me.

Karate

One day, while I felt I was struggling with the memories, flashbacks and helplessness, Dr. Graham suggested that I take a Karate class! He felt it would be good for me to regain some of my power but when he suggested it, my jaw nearly hit the floor. Karate? That was the last thing in the world I would choose to do, which, of course, is why he suggested it. I mean I was the loner; the girl who hid in the back of the room at school; the girl who cut school so she didn't have to give a presentation in class. I was definitely not a Karate student type of person!

I committed to him that I would enroll in the class and I figured by the time the class was scheduled to start, it would be forgotten. Not to be. As happens when you don't want it to, the class had an immediate opening. In fact, the instructor was a friend of Dr. Graham. I cannot describe the fear I had driving to that class. I could not believe I was doing this but if I turned back now, I would be breaking my commitment and I could not bear to disappoint Dr. Graham.

I felt extremely shy and self-conscious because I knew absolutely nothing about Karate. I stood in the back of the class trying to mimic the strange poses and as soon as the class was over, I was the first one to my car. However, the most amazing thing happened – I felt proud of myself for doing it! I was terribly glad the first class was over and I was still petrified of the next one but I had done something that I would never have done before. I had let myself be vulnerable in a good way.

I continued going back each week and learned more and more. Towards the end of the course, the instructor announced that there would be a final exam. This was a college course and I would receive school credits for completing it. I wondered what a final exam for Karate would be.

We had learned different poses, moves and routines. The final would consist of us performing a certain routine from start to finish. The major problem with this final is that we would have to do this in the middle of the room in front of everyone. Panic filled me. I knew I could not do this but I also knew that I had to or I would go back to Dr. Graham as a loser. Loser was my word, of course, but I had come this far and I wanted to finish this.

Besides the overall issue of doing the routine, there was one more thing that scared me. After the execution of certain moves, the climax of the Karate routine was to yell out from your gut. Known as 'Kiai', the yell is a primal release of stored energy, a way of bringing up your internal power. The instructor said that the yelling out would be an important part of the overall grade.

On the evening of the final, I arrived but still felt inside that I wouldn't be able to go through with it. Yet when it came to my turn, I got up and did it. I executed the moves perfectly but I could not yell out at the end. It was just too difficult for me. Just too risky.

When the instructor read out my name for the results, he had given me an A! I could not believe it. I was really surprised. After the class, he told me that when I had first started the class, he knew how scared I was and to be able to do what I did alone, in front of a group of experienced Karate students, was pure bravery to him – even without the yelling at the end.

I felt prouder in that moment than at any other time in my life so far.

Diabetes

The following week, I took Jeni to our doctor after I noticed that she seemed to have developed an unquenchable thirst. Jack told me that his family thought I was being overprotective and paranoid. She was diagnosed with Type 1 Juvenile Diabetes. I was in shock and so scared. What else could go wrong? I didn't want her to have this disease. I had to be brave for her. I didn't know anything about it (only that it was serious and incurable). Within a few days, I knew everything about it and was giving my 8-year-old daughter injections of insulin every morning, afternoon and evening.

I really didn't think too much about what I had to do, I just knew I had to take care of her and help her accept this illness as best as I could. There was never a question of whether I could handle it or not – I had to handle it. I went through a training program to learn about how to give the injections, take the daily blood sugars and monitor her diet. We were stunned to realize it meant a whole new lifestyle for all of us. We couldn't wake up each morning and float through the day. There were injections, blood sugars, urine tests and diet regimens to follow. She was required to eat every 2½ hours to balance the amount of insulin and blood sugar in her system.

She was having a hard time accepting all the changes. She had nightmares of not being able to get to her insulin and it broke my heart. I wanted to have the disease rather than her. It was scary to find out that there wasn't a set daily dose of insulin that we were required to give her and that we were responsible for making adjustments to her dosage based on her blood sugars. I felt as if her life was in my hands.

It was up to me to administer the injections at the time. I hated hurting her but I wanted her alive and well. I hated having to tell her she couldn't have a cookie when all the other kids were having one. The adjustment was hard on her. I was very strong for her and never let her see my fears or worries. I wanted so much for her to adjust to this new way of life so that it would become a part of her everyday living. I wanted her to live a long and healthy life.

At the time all this was happening, more memories and flashbacks were surfacing. I wasn't able to stop them just because I had this other crisis going on in our lives. Dr. Graham took me off the Prozac at this time. He told me he was impressed with the way I was handling my daughter's diabetes and that really made me feel good. I have always seemed to be able to come through for my children. They are everything to me. I had never thought of myself as strong in any way before.

Boundaries

After I had been in therapy for about 3 months, Jack's support seemed to wane. He had thought that I would be "cured" within a relatively short period of time. Neither one of us realized what it would involve even to begin dealing with my abuse. I kept asking Dr. Graham how long it takes to get "better". He would always reply that there was no set time limit. It was very frustrating. I wanted to see results faster and my husband was losing his patience. Unfortunately, while all the details of the abuse were surfacing in my mind, I felt myself pulling away from him more and more, physically and emotionally. I was using all my defenses to deal with all the pain, which felt so fresh. It had to get worse before I could get better.

One aspect of my therapy that was particularly hard for him was that I had to be able to set limits with him, to feel that I had some control over what happened to me. Childhood Sexual Abuse takes away any control you have as a child. Your boundaries are constantly violated. In fact, they don't exist. You are powerless against your abuser.

I began telling Dr. Graham of certain things my husband did to me that involved touching and that made me feel uncomfortable to the point of feeling sick and scared. I wouldn't tell my husband that I was feeling them. I didn't want to hurt his feelings because I felt he had been so 'patient'. Dr. Graham taught me that it was okay to say "no" to anything that didn't feel good to me. He told me that to recover, I needed to gain control again over my body and my feelings. What seemed so confusing was that here I was in therapy trying to be able to be intimate with my husband and the way I was to accomplish that was telling him to not touch me. Any touch, hug or kiss made me cringe. You can imagine that if this was confusing to me, my husband had no way of making any sense of it.

It felt to me that when I needed Jack's support the most, I was losing it. I felt like I was sinking in quicksand and losing the battle. If it weren't for my children at that time, I would have killed myself. It was a feeling that I had over and over again. I wanted to run, run, run and keep running. I would wish so bad that I had never started therapy, never talked about anything. I don't know what kept me going sometimes. I am a very stubborn, strong-willed person in some ways. I am not a quitter and I've always finished things I've started. My therapist once told me that my stubbornness would help me through this and had helped me survive as a child.

It was months before I even told my husband about the sexual abuse. My therapist encouraged me to tell him because it would help him understand but it was so very hard at that time to consider telling anyone. When I finally did tell him as much as I could, he was very understanding. He said that he wished my Dad was alive so he could beat him up.

My life seemed to be one of constant turmoil inside. I was plagued by the images of abuse flashing in my mind and all the feelings of fear and sadness that came along with them. I was trying very hard to be strong for Jeni while she adjusted to the diabetes and I was trying hard to open up to my therapist so that I could get through it all and be happy.

Turning points

I kept having that familiar feeling that I didn't want Jack to think of me as dirty or bad or disgusting. In reality, of course, this wasn't the case, but my feelings were out of my control. I also think it was my way of continuing to keep him at arm's length. I was still very afraid of letting anyone too close and especially of intimacy. I felt that if anyone ever knew the 'real' me, the 'crazy' me, they would drop me immediately. I was very afraid of rejection.

Dr. Graham suggested it might be a good idea for my husband to come with me sometime so he could explain to Jack what I was going through. I immediately rejected that idea. I felt that if Jack came in, Dr. Graham would somehow get him to be more forward with me. I wanted nothing to do with intimacy and if my husband found out that it might be a good idea to start experimenting with closeness, I would no longer be safe. My therapist's office was my haven, my safe place and I was unwilling to risk losing it. Of course, that wasn't what Dr. Graham had in mind at all. He only wanted to explain to Jack that I needed to feel in control and, ironically, he was hoping to get my husband to give me some space so that I didn't feel pursued in my own home. But as usual, my fears caused me to immediately put up my guard and ended up keeping people from helping me.

I was so unhappy. I had such deep sadness that it just didn't seem possible to feel any other way. Why couldn't I let people get close to me and help me? I needed help so desperately but wasn't able to allow it. I think I was afraid to be happy. Happiness had always meant danger or hurt in my life. As a child, my hopes were always torn down and, to survive, I had to give up hope. Hope meant disappointment and I couldn't risk it.

I realized around this time that I was beginning to be afraid to get better. It seemed as if I was resisting moving forward. For one thing, me getting better meant having sex and that petrified me. It meant being alone with my husband and that petrified me. It felt to me that to get through my sexual problem meant being raped all over again.

My therapist would explain to me over and over that no one could hurt me like that again and that I had the power as an adult to say what was okay and what wasn't. But it still scared me. I just wanted to stay right where I was, in therapy with a compassionate doctor, safe from my husband and safe from sex. I realized that I needed to move on but it seemed impossible.

Chapter 11

"The bravest thing I ever did was continuing my life when I wanted to die"

Juliette Lewis

Transference

The dependency on Dr. Graham was getting stronger and stronger. I felt that he began to be more and more like the Dad I never had. He was smart, kind and, best of all, cared about what I had to say. It was scary for me to even think of not having him there to talk to. He became a surrogate father to me and I felt loved and cared about when I was in his office.

I began to feel like I was caught between a rock and a hard place. His job was to help me become independent and gain control of my life but I couldn't imagine ever not coming to his office each week. It scared me to have such strong feelings for him. I tried to hide them and not acknowledge them, but they were there. I was afraid that if he knew how strongly I felt about him, he wouldn't want to see me anymore. I think, unconsciously, I fought getting better because it meant a loss of that relationship. I honestly didn't know how I'd survive if I did not have my therapist. I began to wish all the time that he was my Dad. I can look back now and see all of this happening but, at the time, it wasn't so obvious. I just told myself it was normal to have such a strong bond with a good doctor.

Transference was first recognized by Sigmund Freud who initially believed that he was seeing his patients' resistance to the psychotherapeutic process. I can relate to that as I have spent many hours sitting in therapy unable to speak. Transference exists in many forms but in a therapy context, it refers to redirection of a patient's feelings for a significant person to the therapist. These feelings can be seen in many forms such as rage, hatred, mistrust, 'parentification', extreme dependence, or even placing the therapist in a god-like or guru status. Looking back on my relationship with Dr. Graham, it is clear that I had transferred my feelings of my Dad (and my feelings of what I wanted in a Dad) to him and that it was rapidly becoming a barrier to successful recovery.

Concert

It had been about five weeks since I had been off the Prozac and I was becoming severely depressed once again. One night after I left my session, I completely fell apart. I broke down and couldn't stop crying. I felt so down.

I called Dr. Graham the next day.

During the next visit, we discussed starting me back on Prozac. It takes about 4-5 weeks for it to leave your system, so it was possible that was the reason for my emotional collapse. I began taking it again in the hope that it was what had been making me feel down again, and that now I was taking it again, my mood would improve.

Several months earlier, I had purchased some concert tickets for my husband as a Father's Day gift. I had only purchased two tickets – it was the first time I had actually not included the kids. Of course, when I bought the tickets, six months down the road seemed a long time away and I figured I'd face it when the time came. Well, the time had come and I wasn't ready at all! I was terrified at the thought of going to a concert alone with him.

As the concert date drew closer, I became more and more anxious. I felt sick to my stomach and unable to concentrate. Dr. Graham thought this would be a good opportunity for me to practice how to gain more control over a scary situation. He taught me that the way to make a scary situation tolerable is to make it safe by devising an exit. In other words, if I was able to go to the concert, I needed to identify what my specific fears were and create a situation where I could prevent those fears from becoming a reality. I identified that my specific fears were having to be alone in the car with him, having him hold my hand or put his arm around me. I was very scared of those things.

We devised a plan. I would tell my husband that if I was to go to the concert, he couldn't try to hold my hand or touch me in any way. That made it a little better but there was still the problem of being alone in the car with him – it was an hour and a half long drive! Looking back, this sounds a little weird but we decided I would take my own car. My husband would leave first and then I was to follow separately and see how far I could make it.

We planned a system of rating my anxiety on a level from 1 to 10. As soon as I felt my anxiety level reach 5, I would turn around and go home. If my anxiety subsided on the way home and I felt able to go back, I was to turn around and head back to the concert. I was to experiment with my anxiety and see how much I could handle.

By the week before the concert, I was constantly sick to my stomach. One day, I was ironing some clothes and started thinking about the concert and before I realized it, I had to run to the bathroom and vomit. It was obvious that going to the concert was something I really had no desire to do and I was only going through with it so as not to hurt Jack's feelings. This was a pattern in my life.

The ultimate goal of the evening then became an experiment to see if I could NOT go to the concert (whether I could put my need ahead of not hurting Jack's feelings). I was to go ahead as if I was going and experiment with my anxiety levels and hopefully make it into the concert hall and then see if going that far, I would be able to turn around and leave. It may sound weird, but it felt safe to me and that was what was important. I felt pretty good about it.

When Jack's mother heard about the plan, she blew up. It was not my intention for her to know anything. I felt it was our private business but Jack told her everything. She said it was ridiculous and actually invited herself to the concert! She said that she figured if her son's wife couldn't take care of him, she would have to step in and do it for me. She missed the point entirely, not that it mattered. She called Jack and told him "If Janet isn't going with you, I'll use the ticket and go with you".

After all of the emotional build-up, this felt like a betrayal. I felt that my husband should have said "no way" and told her to "mind her own business". It made me feel that I wasn't ever going to be important enough to him for him to tell his family how he felt and to ask them to stay out of our private life.

He ended up not going with her but it was hard for me to really put my all into the experiment, feeling betrayed as I did. He left first as planned and I left a while after. I was feeling pretty depressed about the whole thing. I made it to Oakland (where the concert was being held) and then turned back. I didn't make it into the complex. I was just too depressed. Anxiety wasn't even a part of it at this point. It turned out his brother had gone with him so even if I had made it, the plan wouldn't have worked.

I felt like a complete failure. I went shopping before I went home (it was part of Dr. Graham's plan for me to do something I really enjoyed after not attending the concert). Shopping was (and still is) my favorite pastime, but I didn't enjoy it much that evening.

Let me explain why this incident was a turning point for us. When I first began therapy, I had told Dr. Graham about all the family conflicts that began at the start of our marriage. Then when Jack's family first found out about my sexual abuse (months into my therapy), they told me they supported me and were glad I was getting help. Jack and I figured I had been wrong about them.

I gave them the benefit of the doubt and I foolishly gave them my trust. When the concert episode came up, their true colors began to shine through. It really opened both our eyes to what really was an underlying source of conflict in our marriage and a necessary ingredient for a happy marriage – trust.

I couldn't trust him if he couldn't stand up for me – plain and simple. I needed to feel as if I was the most important person to him. He was always put in the middle by them, made to choose between me and his family. It became crystal clear that, although the abuse was the cause of most of my problems, this family situation had to be resolved before I could trust my husband. I needed to trust him before I would ever be able to get close to him again.

We talked and talked it over and he would say he understood but it never seemed to sink in. In a very short matter of time, it all blew up in our face. In retrospect, what was about to happen was the best thing that could have happened, but also one of the scariest things I had been through.

Pills

My birthday was in a few weeks. I was not looking forward to it. It was my first birthday without my Mom and I was feeling pretty blue. To make matters worse, my in-laws decided to throw a surprise party for my sister-in-law, Cheryl whose birthday was one day before mine. I wasn't surprised to learn that I wasn't included. They had never thrown a surprise party for anyone in all the years I had known them.

They knew I was going to have a rough birthday without my Mom and it was like a slap in the face and another chance to say "Janet is not part of this family." I told myself it didn't matter but inside it did matter. It hurt. I tried to put up my wall so that it wouldn't hurt, but I wasn't very successful. I was beginning to feel totally beaten in dealing with the abuse, my depression (the Prozac wasn't working as well this time) and with the non-existent support of Jack and his family.

My husband called his brother and told him he wanted me included in the surprise party since my birthday was the next day. I was to pretend to be surprised. Nobody knew that I knew about the "surprise". I felt like it was such a sham – they hadn't included me because they wanted to but because they were forced to. I was extremely anxious the week before the party. I was so depressed at always feeling like the outsider. I don't think I ever missed my Mom more than I did at that moment – all I wanted was to be happy and for people to accept me. I was a little girl again, looking for love and approval and always coming up empty-handed.

Then I did something I had never before done in my life – I took a prescription drug for something other than the reason it was prescribed. I had been to the dentist several months earlier and he had prescribed some 10 mg Valium for me to take for anxiety before my dental visits. I had 20 of the pills as I had never used them for the visits. So, Friday night I decided to take a couple of the Valium hoping to relieve some of the fear.

Saturday morning, the day of the party, Linda, Jack's cousin was taking Cheryl and I to lunch and then bringing us to the party. I took a couple of the pills at lunch because I was still so anxious. They made me feel a little relaxed but I was still nervous. As we shopped, I downed a couple more of the pills. When we got into the car, I took about 3 more.

I knew Jack's Mom did not want me there and I did not know how I was supposed to pretend I didn't know about the party. At the party, I had a drink, which I usually didn't do. The party was a disaster. Jack's Mom and I had words, my brother-in-law ignored me and when I got home, I was really depressed. I took the rest of the pills in the bottle so that I would forget about it all. To me, they didn't seem to be working at all. Jack had no idea I had taken any pills at all.

Sunday, I slept all day, didn't even eat. I claimed I felt ill but it was so nice to sleep and not think about it all. Monday, when I took Jeni to school, I backed into a car. No damage but my judgment was way off. I was very anxious and shaky and shouldn't have been driving. I finally called my husband at work and confessed that I had taken the pills because I had been scared. He told me I should tell my doctor but I was too embarrassed and scared that he'd be mad. What a mess I had created.

I had a scheduled appointment with Dr. Graham that Monday and at his office, the effects of the pills really kicked in. I was extremely relaxed. Dr. Graham commented on that because, usually, I was very tense at my sessions. I made the first mistake of many to come over the next couple of days – I lied to him. I told him that my family doctor had prescribed some pills for pain. I just couldn't admit to him that I had taken Valium for something it wasn't prescribed for. I was so afraid he'd get angry with me and be disappointed in me, especially since he trusted me with the Prozac.

Valium was something my Dad had abused the whole time I was growing up and I felt that I had stooped to his level. My Dad had abused Valium for many years and I associated it with being a "bad" drug.

As often happens, when you tell one lie, it leads to another and another. He wanted to know what the medication was and I lied again, I said I didn't know. Everything just kept spiraling. I left his office at the end of the visit and got to my car and realized there was no way I could drive safely. I could barely walk. I went back to Dr. Graham's office, asked to use the phone but I couldn't get hold of anyone to come and pick me up. My doctor offered me a ride and I accepted but I felt so bad for lying to him. He asked me to come in the next day.

Although I did not realize it at the time, taking Valium to 'shut out the pain' was to be the first of several such abuses of prescription drugs. Only years later have I admitted to myself and to others that I have a problem. As I will recount in this book, I have resorted to overdoses of pills on several occasions – not to die but to shut down. People often think of a Pill Addict as someone who uses prescription pills to 'get high' or who becomes addicted to 'Opiate pain relievers' but I have learned that using prescription drugs for any reason other than that for which they were prescribed is an abuse. I have found myself dependent upon having the pills available 'just in case I need to shut down' and only in the last few months of my journey have I managed to begin working on that unhealthy thinking.

County Mental Hospital

The effects of the Valium were still affecting my motor skills and my judgment. Without my knowledge, Jack had called Dr. Graham the next morning and told him everything. Jack insisted on driving me because it wasn't safe, and I walked into Dr. Graham's office unaware that he knew I had taken all the Valium. He asked me again if I knew what I had taken and when I said no, he made a call and Jack walked into the office! I have never before in my life, ever felt so betrayed by both of them.

Dr. Graham told me that he was going to admit me to the hospital, the County Mental Hospital, which is all that our insurance would cover. He said that I was being admitted to a mental hospital because he felt I was a danger to myself and especially since, unbeknown to me, the Prozac in my system was prolonging the effects of the Valium. It was to be the first of several hospital stays.

I was absolutely terrified of the hospital. I couldn't believe I was actually in a mental hospital. That is where my Dad always ended up after his suicide attempts. I was the smart one of the family, the one who escaped, the one who survived. How did I end up here? I was so scared of the other people. A lot of them were psychotic and I had never seen such things. I was extremely depressed. I couldn't believe what I had done. I didn't eat or drink for 4 or 5 days.

I slept and slept. I had spoken to Dr. Graham on the telephone and I cried for him to come and see me. He said that he was not sure if he would continue working with me. He explained about patient/doctor trust being crucial to a therapeutic relationship. I felt he was abandoning me when I needed him. I knew I had done this to myself, but I felt like everyone was leaving me.

While I was in the hospital, Jack's family was working to convince him to leave me and take my children from me because I was obviously "crazy". He was, again, playing both sides and going along with them while acting like he supported me. I could feel everything working against me and I felt so low. I was there for about a week before the medication had left my system enough for me to be released.

When I got home, my husband and I had a long talk about everything. I told him (again) that I could not live this way any longer – he was either with me or not. I told him that if he was with me, he would have to stand up for me to his family. I had never felt that strong about it before. I told him to make his mind up one way or the other. His Mom had convinced him I would beg him to stay with me and when he heard what I said, he was surprised because I was not begging. He chose me and promised to make a stand with his family for me. It was the beginning of my first real trust towards him.

Promise

The thought of facing Dr. Graham at my next appointment filled me with fear. I didn't know what to expect. I wasn't sure if he was angry or if he had decided not to continue seeing me because of the trust issue. I was also very, very embarrassed. I felt as if I had screwed everything up again. I always seemed to push away any person who cared about or wanted to help me. I was in for a big surprise. He definitely wasn't pleased with what I had done but he told me that he wished I would have been honest with him from the start about the pills and that he would give me another chance. I promised to open up to him and trust him and I kept that promise to the best of my ability.

There were times in the months that followed when I felt the urge to take pills to escape, but I always told him when I was feeling that way. The whole experience was terrifying to me because I never would have dreamed I could get to a point where I felt so low and so much pain that I would turn to pills. It worried me that if I had done it once; I would be tempted to try again.

The experience also had benefits. It seemed to me that since my therapist had seen me at my worst, I really had nothing to hide so I seemed to really be able to talk to him openly most of the time and definitely a lot more than before. Finally, it had also brought the family situation out in the open. Not long afterwards, I finally agreed to have my husband come in with me to therapy.

The flashbacks had eased up a little, but the depression was in full force. The meeting with Dr. Graham turned out very well. He explained to Jack about the effects of Childhood Sexual Abuse and how I needed to feel in control again and, most importantly, he gave Jack hope that I would be able to recover from it all. It seemed to help Jack to hear it all from a doctor's point of view. All in all, things seemed to be looking up.

Little did I know, within a couple of weeks, the worst memory of all would surface and I would go through my darkest period. It seemed that this path to recovery was not smooth and was the hardest road I had ever travelled.

I want people who are reading this who may be going through or have been through similar experiences to feel hope, to know that it is possible to be able to rise above it all and triumph over this monster that tries to destroy our happiness. We had no power as children, but we must remember that we, as adults, have the power to say "no more! I will not let them win"…even if we have to say it over and over again.

Chapter 12

"*I was like a clock that had exploded - my springs were hanging out, my hands were cockeyed and my numbers were falling off.*"

From Scar Tissue by Anthony Kiedis

New Year

Icontinued my weekly therapy visits and as the weeks passed by in the run-up to Christmas, I started having really bad dreams again and images flashing in my head all the time. I felt like the depression was coming back stronger and stronger. While talking to Dr. Graham one night about it all, he pushed me a bit to see if I would talk. It all poured out. All the memories of the rape by my Dad's drug 'friend' on New Year's Eve. All the betrayal, the pain and the fear.

Afterwards, he assured me that I was very brave to let that poison out. He told me that he was worried about New Year's Eve coming up the next week, especially because of the recent overdose of Valium. He suggested that I could be voluntarily admitted to the same mental hospital for safety and I agreed.

The County Mental Hospital was full that New Year's Eve. There were a lot of very sick people there and I felt very scared. I felt scared of them, I felt scared of the night and the memories. I felt scared of everything. I knew then that Dr. Graham had been right and that if I were at home, I would have found a way to take an overdose of pills. So, I curled up into a ball on my bed and tried to sleep the night away.

I remember one very unhelpful nurse that evening who questioned Dr. Graham' motives for wanting me to be there. I just wanted to forget the night and go to sleep but she kept trying to get me up. I told her to leave me alone and turned towards the wall. The flashbacks came full force. The rape, the shame, the disgust and the dissociating feeling, the Dad that did that to me and the knowledge I would never have a Dad to love me.

I told Dr. Graham the next day about the nurse. He asked me how I felt about talking to the nursing supervisors to explain what happened. He said it would give me more of my power back and I agreed. I had a meeting with the supervisor and the nurse about it. I told them how much what she said had hurt, especially since if she had taken the time to read my chart, she would have seen that night why I was there.

In the end, I was in the hospital for two weeks. It seemed like a very long time. I wanted to get out but I was also scared to get out. I didn't trust myself anymore. I felt so fragile. I just didn't know what was happening to me. While I was there, they switched me from Prozac to Trazodone. There was a slight problem with my blood pressure and shakiness but they told me the side effects would diminish.

The New Year I spent in the County Hospital remains a significant event in my mind. I was probably at my most vulnerable then and the dependence upon Dr. Graham had become critically impactful. Reading my journal from that time reminds me not just of how much I was hurting but also how far I have come. How I wish I could go back to me then and teach me some of what I have learned in the last couple of years.

2 January 1993

Why can't I trust anyone completely? Everyone offers help but I always think they will never stick with me. They will see the real me the bad me, the no good ugly part and give up on me.

I wish I could feel different, I want to be happy and trust that someone could actually like the real me. I don't even know who the real me is. I think my so-called Dad destroyed any good in me. I don't care what that stupid nurse said; I don't forgive him and can't forgive him. I hate him for making me this way. And I don't believe Dr. Graham is just out for my money. He seems to really care and yes, I depend on him, but I'm supposed to and yes, I trust his judgment but I need to trust someone. He's right... I am always waiting for someone to drop me but it's because someone always does. I want to feel good about me but I don't. That stupid nurse seems to agree and it hurt me. I can't live like this anymore.

I don't have much fight in me left!!!!! I'm tired and not brave. How could you do this to me Dad?

You've ruined my life!!!!!!!! I hate you. I wish you would have loved me.

Mom could always make me feel better because I know she loved me. I don't have anyone else who loves me that way.

Out and back

After I was released and got home, I felt so shaky – I can't describe how bad it felt, physically and emotionally. I felt so out of touch with my children and what was going on in their lives and could barely function.

I got out on a Monday, saw my doctor on Thursday, and by Friday, I just wasn't handling things at all. I had no patience with the kids, I felt totally on edge and extremely fragile. I called Dr. Graham but I didn't feel like he could do anything for me.

I woke on Saturday morning with the familiar pain and I had an extremely strong urge to run far away from everything. Nothing worked. Therapy didn't help and medication didn't help. I always ended up back in the same place. I felt betrayed, broken and beyond any help. I called my doctor's answering service and left a message that I couldn't take the pain anymore and thanked him for trying to help me. Basically, I said goodbye to him.

I hated that I needed him so much. It seemed as if the compassion he gave me was never enough and he could never prove to me that he cared enough. I always felt like I would lose him and he would become tired of dealing with me and would give up on me. It didn't matter how hard he tried to help me, it never felt as if it was enough or that it would last.

I soaked up all of his concern and care for me. I wanted him to protect me like a father would protect his daughter. The transference monster inside of me prayed, wished and imagined that Dr. Graham was my father and I began wanting that feeling more and more. I wanted a Dad who loved me; I wanted someone to be proud of me, to care about what happened to me. And I believed that was exactly what Dr. Graham wanted for me. I knew that in my heart.

The answering service took my call to be a suicide note and called Dr. Graham immediately. He called the Sheriff's Department and they came out and took me back to the County Mental Hospital. I didn't want to be back there. I felt so trapped and so angry with Dr. Graham for making me go back. He didn't even call me and I felt that he had just thrown me back there. Passed me along. Just like my real Dad had done.

Negative transference occurs when some conflict or blockage prevents a good working relationship. If a client is emotionally stuck on the therapist, it can prevent and distract the real healing from happening.

In my case, my therapist showed genuine kindness, acceptance and compassion, to me and my inner child. My inner child attached to my therapist and I wished with my whole heart that he would be the father I never had. I began to cling excessively to him and pretend he was my Dad. Of course, at the time, while I was in the middle of it, all I could feel was the hurt. I did not understand what was happening. I just knew that I needed him to accept and love me as a daughter or I would die.

He, of course, knew that all of this was happening and what it was doing to me. I would constantly need reassurance from him and if I didn't get it in the way I needed it, I would sink lower into my depression. I began taking more pills, which was not only a way to escape but a way to get his attention and compassion.

Abandonment

One day, Dr. Graham talked to me about transitioning to a woman therapist. He told me that he felt that the therapy with him was not progressing because of the transference issue. He explained it all to me very compassionately but all I heard (and felt) was rejection. The worst rejection of my entire life. I cannot describe the pain. I had found a father who loved and respected me and now I was losing him.

He knew a woman psychiatrist who he wanted me to see and he said that he just wanted me to go see what I thought of her and then to come back and discuss with him.

I went to talk to this woman – Dr. Wright – and although she was nice, it felt so much like starting over and I wasn't sure I could do it. Dr. Graham had given her my history so it wasn't as if I had to go over everything from the beginning but it was so awkward because I didn't know her as a person and she didn't know me as a person. I had truly walked in there wanting to feel comfortable but when I was in there, all I felt was that I wanted to be back in the safety of Dr. Graham's office where I felt at home and safe. I told her all of this and when I went back to Dr. Graham, she had already talked with him.

As soon as I walked into his office, I knew that he had made up his mind about me seeing her and he wasn't going to change his mind. I was angry. I felt like I had no choice. I was trapped. I ask him to explain to me why he thought this change was so necessary. I tried to listen with an open mind and his reasons made sense. I just felt so scared. I had felt he would always be with me to the end and always on my side. I felt as if I wasn't going to have a safe place anymore. I was confused.

I agreed to give her a chance and he agreed to let me come visit him for short visits while I was making the transition. That worked okay the first few times but it became too hard for me to see him, knowing I couldn't really talk about things with him. He wanted me to talk issues over with her now. The truth was that it had to happen and it really wasn't a choice.

The last time I saw Dr. Graham, I was argumentative. I felt like I was losing my best friend. The one "normal" person who had validated my feelings and made me feel like I was normal and who didn't react to me with disgust. The Dad I never had but had finally found. I needed him. I was really hurting inside. I felt as if my heart was breaking. I was frustrated at him because it seemed to be so easy for him to just pass me along. Like I wasn't important.

In my journal at the time, I expressed how I was feeling and the following entry captures it.

I am so very scared - feel like I'm spinning. My head seems to be lifted out of a cloud. Tuesday night, I felt like I was up above my body looking down at myself. I feel like a Tiffany lampshade hanging over concrete - it would take so little to break me for good. Feel like I will never find myself again.

In reality, all these feelings I was having were directly related to my experiences of rejection and low self-esteem but they felt very real to me. On the one hand, I wished I could hate him because then it wouldn't hurt, and on the other hand, I wanted to end it without hating him but that meant a lot of hurt. I really hated my Dad for doing this to me. I felt it was his fault that I was the way I was; always seeking approval and support from a father figure.

I went home that last day with the heaviest grief I had ever experienced. I could not get out of bed and the depression was debilitating. I couldn't be there for my children and I could barely function.

Dr. Wright was such a kind lady who understood and ended up being a lifesaver to me, but I could not get over the pain of not seeing Dr. Graham. This began a path of pill taking, several suicide attempts and a couple of the worst years I have ever had.

I kept a journal, wrote letters and poems pouring out the pain and the abandonment that I felt. I still feel that little girl inside of me fighting for her life. The emotion of what I wrote still washes over me and the hurt of that period in my life still lives with me although I have learned to put it into a box and only open it when I choose to.

It is often said that true recovery cannot start until one reaches 'rock bottom'. For most of my life, I looked upon Dr. Graham's 'abandonment' as my 'rock bottom'. The depth of the grief and the impact upon my emotions cannot be explained with words.

As it turns out, this was not to be my 'rock bottom'. That would not occur for another twenty years.

Changes and treatments

After a short while, I began opening up to Dr. Wright. She was a very kind person and she helped save my life at an awfully painful and difficult time. After several months, she stopped accepting our health insurance plan and I had to find another therapist. I went to someone that she recommended. He ran a group that she thought would be helpful for me to attend.

I liked the group immediately. The doctor and the participants were very kind and it helped to be with people who understood me and had been through similar experiences. As I began to share my story, they showed me such compassion. The doctor thought that it would be a good idea for me to go to a treatment center that was covered under my insurance. He said that it was not a hospital setting but it was a beautiful place where I would be able to be safe and work through this whole experience. I checked out the place; found it was covered under our insurance and it looked peaceful and welcoming to me. I was admitted within a couple of weeks.

Even though our marriage had serious problems by this time, my husband brought our children to see me and I will always be grateful for that. He told me afterwards that my in-laws were again trying to convince him to get a lawyer and to take the kids from me because I was as "crazy" as they had always believed.

My new doctor at the treatment center was another very kind, compassionate man and, unfortunately, the whole transference issue began again. I was starting to feel as if I would never be whole again, that I would never be able to have a Dad that cared and that these surrogates would not be able to replace that. I felt that the pain inside would never go away. I started to give up. I lay in my bed every spare moment, hugging my teddy bear, rocking myself. The facility was not a strict hospital setting and apart from attending group sessions and going on outings, I was in charge of my own day.

I wasn't getting better. I was getting worse. While I was in the community room one evening watching the television, my doctor came and sat by me and asked me to watch a video and to be open to it. I was intrigued and hoped it would help. At this point, I wanted the pain to stop and would consider any option that made that possible.

The video was about Electroconvulsive Therapy (ECT). ECT is a procedure, performed under general anesthesia, in which small electric currents are passed through the brain, triggering a brief seizure. The video explained that ECT causes changes in brain chemistry that can quickly reverse symptoms of certain mental illnesses.

My first thoughts were of the things I had seen on television in the old movies. I was frightened at the thought of it. My doctor said that he did not believe anything else I had tried was helping me and he thought this was worth a shot. He said it had a high percentage of success. I agreed even though I was scared to death (and, of course, I wanted to please him). He explained that short-term memory was a common side effect and I asked him to call me after the first treatment to reassure me that I hadn't lost my entire memory.

When I was admitted to the hospital, I felt like I was in one of those scary mental hospitals that you see on television! After the first ECT session, I woke up and had no idea where I was, who I was and why I was there. I did not like the feeling. Things slowly started coming back and as promised, my doctor called me to assure me I still knew who he was. We had two group sessions each day and everyone was there for the same ECT treatment. I remember sitting in the group feeling confused and not being able to get all my thoughts together properly.

I had two more ECT sessions, followed by similar memory loss and group sessions. During one of the groups, I had talked to one of the other patients about the therapist issues I was still struggling with. He gave me the name of his therapist, saying he was the best therapist he had ever had.

After the third treatment, I was sitting in the group,

struggling with my memory and thinking to myself, "How did I end up here?" I couldn't remember my entire visit at the previous treatment center (including a day out with my kids to see a movie). When it was mentioned to me, I had no recollection of it. I decided then that I had to get back to my kids and be the mother they needed. I had been in a two-year major depressive episode and it was time to take charge of my life. I was discharged the following day and was never so happy to see my beautiful children.

After getting home, I called the doctor who the patient had referred to me. He was a very kind man and, fortunately, I didn't have any transference issues with him. Dr. Harris was like a jolly Santa Claus and I found it easier to talk to him than I had the others before him. The first couple of sessions went really well and I was starting to feel that I was making progress. While going through my history, Dr. Harris mentioned that he knew Dr. Graham and, in an instant, I was consumed again by wanting to find out how he was and whether he still cared about me. Familiar feelings of hopelessness engulfed me and I dropped into a period of pill abuse, suicide attempts and the depression that clung to me like a black cloud.

I even wrote a letter to Dr. Graham as if from the man who had raped me when I was 9 years old. I cut my own throat and then called the police saying that someone had broken in and that I had been attacked. Dr. Graham, concerned for my safety, turned the letter over to the police and they connected it with the phony break-in and brought me in for questioning. Of course, they were quick to determine that it was all of my own making and a woman police officer (who was incredibly kind to me) drove me to County Mental Hospital again to be evaluated.

One of the suicide attempts was very serious and I almost died. Dr. Wright once told me that she knew I really didn't want to die but that one of these times, I was going to accidentally succeed. Things just seemed to keep getting lower each time. If it was not for my children needing me at that time, I do not believe I would be alive today.

I continued to see Dr. Harris, and after some time, I was strong enough to get a job. I worked for a non-profit organization in Sonoma County that helped families with children who were at risk. It was federally funded and I was quickly promoted to a caseworker with about 30 families to manage. I loved the job. Every part of it. I felt like I was doing something to make a difference.

My marriage was crumbling. We both had affairs. When I spoke in therapy about it, we tried to devise plans for repairing it. Nothing seemed to work. My husband suggested that we go to couples' counseling but I was done. I needed to get out of this marriage for all of our sakes. I had no emotion or energy left to try.

Part Two Footnote

When I look back on the five years of my life covered in Part Two, I see myself on an emotional rollercoaster. I experienced some of the most wonderful times of my life, such as the birth of my children and the realization that I was not crazy. I also experienced some of the lowest times as the dysfunction of my childhood continued to drive my emotions and left me exposed to and unprepared for the pain of the journey of therapy and recovery. I still look back on this period as one that contains the very real outcomes of the sexual abuse that I had suffered. Crippling depression and deep pain as the memories flooded my life and the seeds of what was to become a life-threatening issue with prescription drugs.

As I have already said, my relationship with Dr. Graham was especially impactful. The feelings of abandonment when he withdrew from my therapy were as painful as anything that had ever happened to me. I felt that it was my fault that he had to stop our therapy, that I should have been able to say it better, that I should not have taken the pills and been more honest. Of course, this was untrue but, at the time, I felt that I was bad and that no-one would be able to stick with me. My journal entries at the time are full of self-critical comments and expressions of helplessness:

"I just can't seem to function for long periods of time. I never stable out. Maybe his idiot family is right about me. Maybe I am ruined. I wish I wasn't here sometimes. I wish I could vanish and disappear from this world and have everyone forget about me. Maybe they would be happier."

"Why did Dr. Graham give up on me? He said he would help me if it took 10 years. But then he got rid of me when I needed him to care."

"I was just writing in my book and wrote something that I hadn't realized I felt before about Dr. Graham. I felt hurt that it seemed so easy for him to just "pass me along" to someone else. Like he wouldn't even miss me or care how I was doing. My Dad passed me along to his friends as if I was an object and didn't matter."

In the period after, I was encouraged to write my feelings in the form of letters to Dr. Graham (which would not necessarily ever be sent). I have shared these here as they demonstrate my state of mind and the extent of the transference better than I can describe it. What strikes me reading these now, is how desperately I craved love and approval from my Dad and how Dr. Graham had become that replacement in my mind.

Dr. Graham,
    You are part of this whole process. I can't just turn off my feelings for you or pretend like you don't matter because you do. I just have to get the intensity of those feelings into some perspective and reality. That's the hard part. One way I feel I can do that is to get everything off my chest that I need to tell you and then try to let go a little more. I think if I don't write you for awhile it will help. Right now, I'm still too tempted to tell you about everything that's going on in my life when I know I need to really rely totally on Dr. Wright for that.
    I've talked to her about all of this. When I write to you again I want it to be for the right purpose of sharing some good news about my progress with you. Part of me says you don't care what happens to me anymore but the smart part says you wouldn't have done all you done working with me if you didn't care. I want and you want me to get better. I have constant battles with myself about this. One minute I think you don't care and then the other minute I'm mad and then the other minute I miss you. It's crazy. I've got to give myself some time to start letting the feelings out and put them where they belong.
    A lot of the feelings are because of my stupid Dad. I know you're not my Dad, but sometimes it feels that way. What's confusing is you're nothing like my Dad. I hated him. Dr. Wright says it's because you're everything he wasn't and I love and I look to you to fill that void and it's impossible because you're not my Dad. It's a loss I'll have to mourn and learn to live without. But it doesn't

have to be all or nothing. I want to work through
these feelings so one day I can feel like even
though you can't fill that void, you can still care
about what happens to me.

It seems like I feel as soon as I'm out of
someone's site or reassurance I feel they don't
care anymore. What a mess! Dr. Wright feels totally
sure I'll get through all this. You always said I
would too. It seems hard to me but I'm going to try
my best.

Janet

Dear Dr. Graham,

I'm going to write you when I feel like talking
to you because I think it will help me get through
the tough times. I have times where I miss you so
much. I'm not going to mail them, but maybe one day
I can look back on them chronologically and read
my progress. Lately I've been missing you a lot.
Sometimes I'm really okay with that like when I
sent you that letter. Then all of a sudden I want
to talk to you so badly. You gave me such a feeling
of compassion and safeness. I've never felt that to
the extent I did with you. You could always make me
laugh and sometimes you would get me so mad and I
would think I was hiding it and I realize you knew
it all along. And sometimes you egged it on. I feel
like I love you like a father. Right now, I don't
know if I'll ever stop feeling that way.

I don't think I'll ever stop caring about you.
I hope I can get a lot better at controlling the
intensity of my feelings for you. I'm jealous of
the people who get to talk to you. I think that's
one of the hardest things about working at my new
job, so close to you, knowing that you were seeing
other people and giving them the comfort that I
want from you. It makes me feel like you forgot
about me. At the same time, I'm so grateful to you
for making this change because maybe I will be able
to progress faster. It feels like I'm not going
anywhere sometimes but I think I really am. You
would be really proud of me and my job. I'm doing
a really good job and they're really pleased with
my work and they really think I'm smart and they

like me. I get so much from this job. I've thought
a couple of times about leaving because it so hard
to be so close to you, but this job is too good for
me. I need to find a way to make it work and I will.
I hope you're doing okay. I really missed talking
with you as you are so smart. You really made me
feel smart too. Well I'm going to go now.
Janet

Dear Dr. Graham,
This is one of the hardest letters I've had to
write, but I feel it is necessary for me to write
it so I can move on. I know I've written you a
lot in the last four months. I also realize that
I really haven't let go of you yet. So here I sit
four months down the road, just now realizing that
somehow I have to find a way to let go of you in the
capacity I had you for almost a year. You were a
confidant a great teacher and someone always on my
side. I need to move on without losing the goodness
of the therapy. I want to take all the things you
taught me and use them to have a happy life and I
need to take the feeling that you do care about
what happens to me.
Dr. Wright says that I don't seem to be able to
feel that people care about me once I leave or when
I have bad days. It's like it erases all the good.
Another area for me to work on.
I will always always care about you and I will
always be happy for my first experience in therapy.
I had one of the best. As I write this it hurts
like Hell because I feel as if it's taken me all
the time since I stopped seeing you to get strong
enough to let go. I have to do it. I know you
understand. I hope you understand also that the
letters I've been writing have been a tool for me
to get to this point.
You've left me in very good hands with Dr.
Wright. I'm going to try hard to put my whole self
into my therapy with her now. She's been so helpful
in working through my feelings for you. She says
when my work with her is done, I will feel more
of a closure with you and at that time it will be
appropriate to give you a call, not for therapy or

because I need to see you but because I'll hopefully be at a point to show you the new me the happy me.
   Janet

Dr. Graham,
   I am not going to mail this letter but I am going to write you in this journal when I need to talk to you. I am going to try and get my feelings for you under control. My feelings are so strong for you that they really get in my way which of course is why you had to stop seeing me. I do see why that was necessary even though I don't like it and it hurts really bad. I miss you so so much. Sometimes I feel like you have forgotten about me or that you're glad you don't have to deal with my problems anymore. But deep inside I know that's not true. So, I am going to try and remember all the positive things you told me.
   You told me you weren't rejecting me and even though it feels like that a lot of the time, I know it's just because of my past that I feel that way. My stupid Dad screwed a lot of things up for me. My Mom didn't help either. I'm starting to realize that that is where the intensity of my feelings for you are coming from. You are such an opposite of my Dad. I would have given anything to have had a Dad like you who listened to me and cared about me. But like you've told me many times, you're not my Dad and I won't ever have a Dad like that. I know you do care about what happens to me but you can't fill that deep void that I have in me and I realize what you were trying to tell me when you told me it was getting in the way of helping me.
   I think it's going to take me a while to sort it all out but I think when I can get over this hurdle and work through these confusing feelings about my Dad I will be ready to take care of the rest of the issues I have too. I'm just now starting to understand what you meant when you tried to explain it to me. I was and have been so emotional over leaving you, feeling hurt one minute, mad the next and then missing you like crazy the next. It's so crazy but I've been thinking about what I need to do to get through this and one thing I am going to

do is not write you for a while. It's kind of hard because I want to talk to you all the time about everything that's going on but I need to separate from that more so that I can rely on Dr. Wright totally. I think you would want me to do that.

Otherwise I write you and then feel bad when you don't write back even though I know you won't because I need to break away from you more so I can be strong on my own. I know that's what you would want. It's hard but I know I can do it. I'm going to stop beating myself up for that last visit I had with you. I was so argumentative but I know you understand and know that I didn't mean to be that way. I'm going to try hard to remember all the good help you gave me. We did some pretty tough work together. I still have a hard time believing those things happened. I had no idea when I first saw you that all this junk was in me. As hard as it was, I'm glad you were the one I told. You made me believe like I could make it and I will.

You know, sometimes I still remember the way you could get me to laugh when I felt awful! I still laugh sometimes when I think of things you said. I always try to keep a sense of humor. I laugh all the time when I see that orange truck that never moves!! I know you got more than you bargained for with me but I really know you're rooting for me. I will carry that with me when I need it. Please understand that I needed to tell you these things for my own progress. I really believe you know all of this. I think you know me better than me sometimes. It's just for me to go on I needed to tell you these things. When I first left you and I wrote you that letter I was far too caught up in the emotions. I'm just now beginning to sort it all and figure out what I have to do to move on.

As hard as it is for me, I have to let go of you for now. I haven't really done that yet. I still want to write you periodically to let you know when I make progress but I'm not going to write for a while. Not until I've worked through these feelings I have about you and my Dad more. It's too hard. Hopefully the next time I write to you I'll have lots of good news about my progress. I told you the *last time I saw you that after all the hard work we did I want to share in the good things that happen because of all that work and when that happens I will write to you. I am hoping one day I will get to a point where I can think of you and feel happiness about all we accomplished rather than feeling such sadness and rejection that I lost you. I want one day to be able to call you and say I've climbed to the other side of the mountain and I will be able to come see you as a healthy happy person who gets her strength from inside rather than from everyone else.*

By the way I started writing my story in a very rough draft form. But I wanted to kind of get things up to this point - kind of like the first half. I figure when I'm through the rest, I will write the second half. Like you offered, when I am all done with everything and I get the second half written, I want you to read it and I want you to help me with the psychological perspective on the ways my past has affected me and with some of the dream interpretations. I know that is way down the road but as I was writing I realized it could be a really good book, and really help someone.

Janet

Part Three:
Don't Expect Me To Die

Chapter 13

"Just when the caterpillar thought life was over, it became a butterfly."

Author unknown but attributed to Chuang Tzu, 4th Century BC

Simon

Just before Christmas 1995, Jack and I filed for divorce. We continued to live together as we worked through the inevitable practicalities of separating. My job and the kids consumed my time and it was pressure from them that made me buy a computer for Christmas. Back then, the World Wide Web barely existed and the Internet was dominated by 'closed' sites such as CompuServe and AOL. For me, the whole world opened up – it was like being able to connect with people for the first time – people who had no idea about my background and my struggles. I joined forums online where I could talk to other people about things we had in common and I felt a freedom I hadn't felt in a long time, if ever.

I was in a literary forum one night and began chatting with a really funny and kind man. His name was Simon. We seemed to click instantly and talked for hours that first night. He seemed genuinely interested in what I had to say and it was easy to share, although I didn't go into details about much of my history. At one point in the conversation, Simon asked me "who hurt you so badly that you cannot trust me?" I cannot even remember what we were talking about that caused him to say it but it has stuck with me ever since. Somehow, he has always had the ability to sense what I am feeling and the barriers that I spent years building up seem not to work with him!

This was in the days before all of the dating sites existed and it was still considered dangerous to connect with anyone personally online. They could be an axe murderer!

The day after Simon and I talked, I felt like I was walking on air. I knew that this man was special. He seemed to be everything I had ever dreamt about but did not think existed. Kind, smart, intelligent, funny and I wanted to know him more. Unfortunately, he lived in New Zealand (a long way from California). He was also in a marriage that was coming to an end and may soon be moving back to England (his home country) so that his wife and their children would be near family.

Over the next few months, we continued our 'accelerated pen friendship', chatting online, emailing, swapping photos and progressing to talking on the phone. At each stage, our connection just grew stronger and the more I shared of my life, the more I found Simon accepting me for who I was. He said that however horrific my experiences had been, they had made me the person I am and that is who he was falling in love with. Nothing I said (or have ever said) to him has changed how he treats me and, although it has taken a long time, he knows everything about me and my experience and loves me more as a result. The complete opposite to the first half of my life.

We continued to talk, email, and send pictures and after a couple of months, we were able to meet while he was on a business trip in California. Meeting in person for the first time felt like we had already met and known each other forever. I knew in my heart we were meant to be together and I felt truly happy for the first time since my Mom had died. By the time we actually met face-to-face, I was divorced, had moved with the kids to my own apartment, I had my job, my own life and freedom. I began to feel like I had a future.

A wedding

Within a year, we were living in England. Both of us went through very difficult processes to be together. My kids were not allowed to come with me (a combination of practicality, immigration and family) and, although it was painful beyond description to be away from them, we had to agree to them staying with Jack in California. Simon and I needed to work on immigration issues for both of us so that we would be able to live in both places. We did manage to get back to California a couple of times to see the kids and they came to

England but being apart was incredibly painful for me and, to this day, I live with the guilt of leaving them. Even with the pain of the separation, however, I was happier than I had ever been and things were looking up.

Within another year, Simon and I were married. The ceremony was in England with all five of our children at the wedding. It was a magical day and one that I did not think was ever possible for me.

I had found my Prince. We are soul mates in every way. I had never felt this loved, cared for and cherished before. We wanted to spend every minute together and I knew that we would be together forever.

Another move

We began to work on Simon's immigration so that we could move back to the US, find work and be able to both live in both places. It was desperately heartbreaking to be away from any of our children but, despite the agonies we each have felt, in the end we all became a wonderfully close, blended family.

When I had first moved to England, I had to stop my therapy and all of my medication (Dr. Harris had swapped me onto Effexor which had been helping me manage but the side effects of stopping were not pleasant). I had no medical coverage in England and the lack of therapy and medication took their toll. I had ups and downs and the downs were really low again. As well as the familiar bouts of depression, I started to experience much stronger PMS which would pretty much change my personality for a couple of weeks every month.

While we worked through the preparations to move back to the States, my children were suffering pretty badly. My son Jason, who was 9 years old when I left, wasn't doing well at school because of the emotions of us being separated. One visit when I went to see them, he broke down knowing that I had to leave again. I will never lose the pain of that. It hurts today as strongly as it hurt then.

Jeni, who was almost 12 years old when I left, had begun spending all of her time with a friend from school. She had been enduring a lot of emotional pressure from her Dad. He called her names and told her she was just like me - a whore and a liar and a cheat. She came to England for a while and went to school there but in the end it was too difficult for her being in a different country and she chose to go back to her Dad's in California. Soon after returning, things continued to be difficult and she started smoking pot and, as it does, she progressed into more and more dangerous drugs.

Rehab

After all the immigration was finally in place for us to live in the US, we had another extremely heart-wrenching move. No matter how many times we do it, moving from one country to another is a process of heart-wrenching goodbyes. We ended up in Redwood City, California where Simon got work in Silicon Valley. Jeni, who was now 15, came to live with us. She went to High School there and my son, still going to school near his Dad, came to stay with us most weekends. We were fortunate enough to be able to fly the kids from England to see us and for a while, things were good.

During that first year there, Jeni became very moody and changed a lot. At first, we put it down to her 'being a teenager' but her new friends drove new luxury cars and, it turned out, had supplies of all kinds of drugs. She went to raves and cut school. Her grades fell and we lived in constant fear for her safety – drugs and alcohol do not mix well with Type 1 Diabetes. We did most of the things that parents do when their kid becomes an addict – some of it helped and some of it enabled. We were new to the problem and how I wish we had known then what we know now about dealing with loved ones in addiction. As it was, we watched helplessly as she self-destructed and we were powerless to stop her.

We searched for help and were lucky to get connected to a wonderful police officer from the Redwood City Family Unit.

He helped us see that we needed to make the tough decisions that our daughter was not able to make. He helped us get her admitted to Daytop, a residential boot camp treatment center. She was there for a year and we did everything we could do to support her. We joined (and ended up leading) their family organization and volunteered on holidays, cooking turkeys and potatoes for over 100 people! After a year and after a lot of emotion, fear and bravery, she came out sober and healthy. She has been clean ever since.

Although we did not understand at the time, our ability to help our daughter was hampered by codependence. The trauma of my childhood had hampered my ability to maintain effective boundaries and I found it difficult to see beyond wanting to protect my daughter – even when it was clear that we were, in fact, enabling her. This has continued to be an issue for me – it has taken a lot of work to understand that my childhood led to a lot of emotional immaturity and that my own experiences gave me a view of relationships that is not quite as it should be. Only by understanding that the trauma of my childhood has been shaping my life in so many ways, can I start to 'retrain' myself to more healthy thoughts and more functional relationships with those I love. Luckily, with Jeni, between Simon and I, we managed to get her into a recovery environment which provided exactly what she needed in order to regain her life.

Arizona

During our time in Redwood City, the impact of my menstrual cycle upon my emotions continued to affect our lives. At times, I became deeply depressed and for two weeks out of every month (always starting ten days before the start of my period), I would become a different person – irritable, negative and extremely defensive. After a long series of tests, I was diagnosed with PMDD (Premenstrual Dysphoric Disorder) and was prescribed a very high dosage of Prozac which controlled the symptoms, leveled my emotions and lessened the mood swings. It was the first time I had been back on antidepressants for several years.

After about a year and a half, Simon was asked by his employer to relocate to Scottsdale, Arizona. Despite our first reservations at living in the "desert", we adapted quickly. The area was surprisingly green and beautiful and we fell in love with the incredible landscape. It was exciting and felt like a fresh start with everyone and everything.

We had not taken anything financial from our divorces. We let our spouses pretty much have everything because we did not want long, drawn-out battles over possessions or money. The corporate relocation to Arizona gave us the chance to buy our first house together. It was a very happy time.

We were in Arizona for 7 summers and during that time we had a lot of love, laughter and tears. Our children in England came to visit a lot and they liked AZ too. We went on road trips, small vacations with the kids and all was well. I found a psychiatrist there who was extremely kind and caring and he continued to prescribe my medication.

As life does, the stability was bound to get disrupted and, after about 4 years there, three of my siblings moved to AZ. At first, that seemed nice but all too soon, the family legacy that I had escaped was back. To our surprise, my brother, Ryan, who we partnered with in a remodeling company, was doing heavy drugs and drinking excessively. My brother, Daniel, and his wife moved to be near him and tragedy always followed closely behind, as it always seemed to with my family.

Daniel's wife, who suffered with a brain aneurysm, died from a seizure while drying her hair. He discovered her there at the sink, with the dryer still going, when he got home from work. He had loved her for a very long time and was devastated at the loss. We attended her funeral and saw Ryan – we had not been talking for some time after we had fallen out over how the remodeling company was being managed. We did not speak beyond a simple 'Hello'. It was the last time I saw him alive.

A week after her funeral, Ryan died of an overdose of drugs and alcohol at the age of 41.

His death brought home to me the futility of 'falling out' and I felt extremely saddened at the fact that Ryan and I had not talked for several months. My concerns about how he was running the business seemed a poor reason to lose a brother – especially as he had been out of our lives for so long just a few years earlier. We paid for and planned his funeral and when I got there, the similarity to my Dad's and my eldest brother's funerals was shocking. It was largely made up of young people who Ryan had dealt and done drugs with.

After he died, we took over the running of the business. Simon took a sabbatical from his job and we gave it a good try. Unfortunately, this was at the beginning of the economic downturn in 2007 and the business was struggling to meet its bills as people cut back on the non-essentials. We thought we could get the business back and save the employees' jobs, so we took out a Small Business Administration loan. As it turns out, this was very unwise. The business eventually folded and left us with a mountain of personally-guaranteed debt. We are still paying that small business loan and our wages are garnished to the maximum amount allowed.

When it became obvious that the remodeling company was not on a path to success, we decided to try and sell the business before it became impossible. Our aim was simply to sell at a price that would resolve most of the debt and we were fortunate to find a couple of investors who were looking for exactly that kind of opportunity and who were ready and willing to buy at our asking price.

The business was owned 50% by us and 50% by my brother and because he had died intestate, it was necessary to obtain letters from my remaining brothers and sisters agreeing to the sale. They said no. They thought we were hiding vast fortunes from them and stopped the sale. The assets of the company did not even cover all of the debt and when the reality of this finally dawned on them, they decided that Simon and I must have cheated somehow and, with the exception of one sister, none of them has talked to either of us to this day.

I cannot help but feel that the dysfunction of our childhoods contributed to trust that someone would not be trying to steal from under their eyes. I was hurt deeply by this. My siblings were like my "children" and they all turned on me with their greed.

Simon was contacted by someone he used to work for, offering him a job in North Carolina. As much as we loved Arizona, the business with my family there had tarnished it and we were happy to move to a new adventure and escape the stress.

Chapter 14

"Healing is a matter of time, but it is sometimes also a matter of opportunity."

Hippocrates

North Carolina

In North Carolina, things started off well. Getting away from the stress that Arizona had become was an incredible relief and our lives settled back into a comfortable pattern. We made some good friends there and we even enjoyed the different seasons.

After being there for about a year, in 2008, the company my husband worked for filed for bankruptcy protection and he was burdened most days by the unenviable need to lay off people who had been working there for many years. All of them lost not only their job – with little notice or severance – but also the pension that they had counted on. It was very demotivating for him.

That same year, my husband and I also renewed our wedding vows. We had been married for 10 years and had always wanted to have a big party to celebrate (especially since we had not had any friends at our wedding in England). A lot of our family and friends attended and it was one of the happiest days of our lives. If Simon's Mum had been able to be there, it would have made it perfect but she had died after a short illness just two months earlier.

The month after the Vow Renewal, I had a few female health problems and had to have a full hysterectomy. It was a long recovery after major surgery but it definitely resolved the pain I had been having and, as a benefit, instantly eradicated the debilitating PMDD that had been making my life so difficult for so many years.

Another year had passed and we were enjoying our life despite the health issues and the work stress. The effects of the trauma of my childhood were still affecting me but I had no way of recognizing them. Looking back now with the knowledge I have gained, I see signs of shame and evidence that my reactions were rooted in what had happened to me as a child. It is the reality of Childhood Sexual Abuse that, however awful the actual events of the abuse are, it is the ongoing impact of the trauma that does irrevocable damage. Only by recognizing and dealing with that trauma can the bondage of the experience be released.

Cancer

In October 2009 while we were on a weekend trip to the Outer Banks of North Carolina, I mentioned to Simon that I had been having some strange symptoms the past few weeks. My bowels felt different and I could see a dark blood most days. I promised him that I would make an appointment with our doctor when we got home.

As soon as we got back that Monday, I made an appointment with my primary physician. After an exam, which showed definite blood, I was referred to a gastroenterologist for a colonoscopy. It was two weeks before my 50th birthday and so it was almost time to have one anyway. I really wasn't that nervous. I knew there would be a good explanation for the symptoms.

When I woke up after the colonoscopy, I had a feeling there was something wrong. I had been there with Simon when he had had his colonoscopy and the doctor had come right in to say that everything was fine. While I was lying there, I could see the nurses talking but they weren't coming in to tell me I could leave like they had with my husband. Finally, I saw the doctor walking down the hallway towards us carrying the results and I was relieved. This was more like it. He would show us the pictures and we could get out of there!

When he walked into the room, I instantly had a bad feeling. He told us that he had found a "most likely" malignancy in my colon. They would be sending out the biopsy, but either way, the malignancy had to come out so he referred us to a surgeon. He said he was sorry. The pictures were so ugly. It didn't look good and I felt the world freeze. I felt a single tear roll down my cheek. I felt in shock but still felt inside that this was not that serious.

We went to the surgeon on Thursday and he said even without the confirmed biopsy results, he had seen enough malignancy to know this was a bad one. He wanted to do surgery right away but as the next day was Friday, I would not have time to 'prep' and, although he had a full schedule on Monday, he would fit me in. The seriousness of it started to sink in and I let our children and close friends know what was happening.

We reported to the hospital Monday morning – just a week after we had first talked about the symptoms. That was when the fear and reality of the situation really took over. While I was being rolled on the gurney to the operating room, tears just flowed down my face. It was like all the emotion was finally leaking from my heart.

When I woke up, the doctors were there and they told me that the surgery had gone well but when they had gone in laparoscopically to where the cancer was identified, it wasn't there! Evidently, when having my hysterectomy the year before, my colon had twisted. This meant that my cancer was not where they thought it would be and the diagnosis was switched from colon cancer to the more troublesome rectal cancer. Rectal cancer is considered riskier than colon cancer because there are less barriers to contain the cancer.

He told us that he had removed all of my Sigmoid Colon and had made a resection that was extremely tricky and I was lucky that I was able to avoid a colostomy. Colostomy! I hadn't even realized that had been a possibility! I felt very grateful and realized how fortunate I was to have had the doctors I had during this whole experience. I had the best and will forever remember their compassion and dedication.

If healing really is a matter of opportunity, I feel blessed that we found ourselves in North Carolina when I had my hysterectomy and the cancer. We found the most incredible level of healthcare and were genuinely blessed with an incredible Family Doctor, surgeon and oncology team.

Our family doctor called my cell phone while I was lying in the hospital bed not long after the surgery because he had just got the results of my colonoscopy. He hadn't even realized I was in the hospital. That is how fast they moved and I will be forever grateful that I had the team I had. I was told after surgery that they had got good margins taking out the tumor and were sending tissue for biopsy to see if there were any lymph nodes affected.

An oncologist came in to meet with me and I think the reality of the whole thing was still sinking in. Everything had happened so fast. I had an oncologist? He staged the cancer saying it was probably days before spreading. He recommended a course of chemotherapy and radiation to ensure that there were no cancer cells missed.

What a week! When I was able to go home, I started the chemo right away and I just did what I had to do. I really didn't have any more fear or anxiety. When the chemo and radiation treatment started, I dealt with the effects and the burns as a matter of fact. I received a call from the gastro doctor telling me he was happy to hear that the surgery had been successful. He told me that with the pictures he had taken of the cancer and with the fact I had also had several other pre-cancerous polyps, he had truly believed it had spread. Again, the gratitude overwhelmed me and I felt so very fortunate to be alive.

Simon took the best care of me that anyone could have possibly done. This whirlwind of an experience had deeply affected him as well. The fear of losing your soul mate was something he had not had a chance to really process. He was so strong for me and went with me to every single treatment. I was very ill from the treatments but after it was finished, I got the all clear and we were both very relieved.

I have lived past the five years that have the highest rate of recurrence, so I breathe a little easier now. The fear of recurrence is always there though, the worry that just one cancer cell made it out and is there waiting to strike. The odds of this decrease as each year goes by and I still have more frequent checkups and colonoscopies.

In the course of understanding how my childhood trauma has affected my whole life, I came across research that established links between early trauma and illness in later life. Although I do not make the direct association between what happened to me as a child and my cancer, I do believe that there are 'side effects' of childhood trauma that leave the survivor more open to various health issues later.

Chapter 15

"My fear of abandonment is exceeded only by my terror of intimacy."

Ethlie Ann Vare

New Jersey and new challenges

While in the treatment phase of the cancer, I really didn't feel any fear or overwhelming emotions. It was just a matter of getting through each day. After the treatment finished, however, I began to have real emotional reactions. I felt like I had escaped death but it had shown me how fragile life really is. I had this feeling of wanting to live every minute of life to the fullest and, unfortunately, that driving need inside of me led me to do things I wouldn't have normally done.

I got involved in a friendship and relationship that wasn't healthy for my marriage or me. It was a long-distance relationship and so I felt it was safe and that perhaps life was just about living and loving everyone and everything. It was a feeling I still find difficult to explain.

This attitude caused me to want to be more independent and because I was so different than I had been before the cancer, it caused strain in my relationship with Simon. We had never had anything come between us, not ever, not even close and this distance was so upsetting to both of us but I couldn't stop myself. I started doing things on my own, little things like not going to bed at the same time, not wanting any nurturing; instead, it felt like suffocation. Part of this was a setting of healthy boundaries but I took it to an extreme.

The friends I made were encouraging that independence and telling me that I needed to be my own person. I couldn't stop myself from becoming this different person.

In 2010, Simon was offered a job by one of the companies that purchased a large portion of his old company during the bankruptcy. We had to move to New Jersey, so we put our house up for sale. We rented an apartment in the middle of downtown Morristown and were there for a couple of years. During this time, the distance between Simon and I started to grow. He was in a very unsatisfying job and the work stress was greater than ever. I was in the middle of this change in me that confused and scared me even while I protected it for dear life.

I saw a couple of therapists there but I never really clicked with any of them. My cancer screenings were going well, all coming back clear and despite the tensions, Simon and I did enjoy our time there and had a lot of tremendously fun times.

Jeni had a little girl while we were there and I began to fly regularly from New Jersey back to Arizona to see them. I was completely in love with that tiny little girl from the minute I saw her. It was life-changing.

Going back to Arizona for visits made us miss the West Coast so much. We decided that we really weren't happy on the East Coast. We had loved the times in New York and the entire experience was fabulous, but after returning to Arizona a few times, we really longed to go back to where we were happy and to be near the kids.

Our house took over a year to sell. We finally had to get out from under it and lost all the money we had put into our real estate those past years. We had to sell just about everything we could and cash in all of our retirement to be able to sell the house some $200k below what we owed on it. On top of the devastating losses, we also continued to have to support the repayment of the remodeling company debt. It was very disheartening to lose everything, after we had started over from the bottom again following our divorces.

Arizona and more cancer

On one of the trips to Arizona, we looked through a couple of new housing developments and were surprised at how inexpensive the homes were. Houses were selling for half of what they had sold for when we lived there. We made a decision that we wanted to move back, and we found a house and managed to get enough to put a deposit down. It wouldn't be ready for several months as it was being newly built so we had time to get things sorted in New Jersey.

A few months before we were to move, I planned a trip to see my daughter and granddaughter. I could not seem to go very long between visits! A week before the trip, I went to a dermatologist to see about getting a mole removed. While I was there, I had a yearly skin check. She took a biopsy of one of my moles and had it sent out to the lab. I had had a few skin biopsies in the past but they were never anything serious so I had no worries.

While I was in Arizona enjoying my time there, I was excited to drive by the house that was being built for us but when I got back to my daughter's apartment, I had a voicemail from the dermatologist in New Jersey asking me to call back immediately. She told me that the biopsy of the mole they had sent out had come back and confirmed it was a Melanoma. My insides froze again. My first thought was that I was obviously destined to get every kind of cancer and my life would be cut short.

Since we were moving to Arizona in a couple of months, we decided I would get established with a dermatologist there and have the surgery. After the surgery, they advised me not to travel for a while and Simon and I agreed that I would find an apartment to rent while the house was being built. He packed up the apartment in New Jersey and when he got to Arizona, I was never so glad to see anyone in my life. He worked from home during that time and we drove over to check on the progress of our new house almost every day.

The Melanoma had shaken up the cancer fear inside of me again. I was hypersensitive to any mole for fear of skin cancer and any bowel change convinced me that my rectal cancer had returned. I began to feel some of the old depression coming back but I was able to push it down.

Jeni had another little girl! Simon and I were over the moon and happy to be back in Arizona with the perfect weather, the wide clean roads and near all of our favorite West Coast places. It was a very happy time.

The only threat to us was that I had kept up the long-distance relationship I had started while in North Carolina and it was very unhealthy. He lived overseas so it felt safe. He made me feel adored, intelligent and special and though I loved Simon with all my heart, I felt the uncontrollable need for this other relationship too.

The thought of not having it made me feel that I would die. I felt so very guilty every time I talked to him. He was very critical of my life, of Simon and I, and of me personally but I needed his approval nonetheless. As much as I made excuses not to talk to him, it became a cycle that soon began to take the happiness away that I had felt being back in Arizona.

We loved our new home, having been able to customize it how we wanted it. We loved the space and felt so excited when we moved in. We enjoyed decorating it and Simon designed the outside areas like those in a magazine. To this day, we adore this home and I would be happy to live here forever.

My son, Jason, who still lived in California was having a difficult time with his Dad. Things were so expensive there and he felt he would never get ahead. We told him that we would be happy for him to come stay with us for a while if he wanted to move back to Arizona, and after some thought, he decided to go for it. He packed up and moved in with us.

One of Simon's sons and his wife had been working on getting their Green Cards for years. It is a long, drawn-out process filled with disappointments but they didn't give up. During the process, they were able to come and visit us for weeks at a time and we lived hoping for the day when they would be able to come and not have to leave.

Things seemed much better, but even so, I just couldn't let go of this other relationship. I was tired of the deception and the lies I had to tell just to make time to talk to him (even though I had promised Simon that I would not talk to him again).

Love Addiction

The cycle of deception, guilt and frustration continued and I started getting more and more depressed not knowing how to get out of it. I started talking about it to my psychiatrist and although he helped me talk through some of it, he referred me to a woman therapist in his office who he felt might be able to help more.

After talking to her and telling her everything I was feeling, she identified what I was feeling as symptomatic of the Love Addiction/Love Avoidance process. When she explained it to me, it made sense and I was able to associate with almost all the symptoms. I saw her a few times and she showed me that the way we approach love and affection is heavily driven by the way we developed as children and the experiences we had. Love Addiction and Love Avoidance were common outcomes of an emotionally immature childhood – the result of not having functional and healthy experiences that teach us to set appropriate boundaries on our relationships. She taught me that the trauma we suffer as young children gets 'stored' and continues to affect us in later life. I found this incredibly powerful and for the first time, I could see that the experiences I had had were still impacting my life.

She told me about a treatment center in Arizona called The Meadows. Often referred to as a rehabilitation facility, they specialize in identifying and addressing trauma that lies beneath the problems of depression and addiction. It sounded really hopeful and she said she could call them right away and talk to her contacts there. That sounded good but I told her I was not quite ready for what it meant. It would mean the end of my long-distance relationship and I felt like I would die without that. I would have no other outlet to be able to get this love and approval that I still searched for.

In reality, I had Simon who was ready and willing to do whatever he could to help me through this. This was genuine unconditional love and that made me feel even guiltier because he knew what it was all about and he was still willing to help me through it. He tells me now that he knew it wasn't the real me – that it was some part of me taking over that did not ever seem to be satisfied. Neither of us realized then that it was the deep trauma and shame that could no longer be contained.

To illustrate how deep the trauma bond and love addiction can be, when Simon initially found out about this relationship, he was so deeply hurt and he asked me not to talk to that man again. I agreed but even as I said the words, I knew I couldn't do it. It was horrible to need something so much, but at the same time, I was feeling an unbearable hurt inside for having hurt Simon this way. It was so confusing – I felt like I would die without the other relationship, even though I knew it would never come to anything and that I loved Simon more than anything and would never leave him. I stopped going to the therapist because I didn't want to deal with this right now. It was way too scary.

Simon and I started to see a therapist for couple's counseling. He was a very kind man and was quick to identify that some of the things I was experiencing were part of what he called 'Shame Attacks' and that they were a direct result of the trauma of my childhood (not just the sexual abuse but the continued dysfunction that had prevented me from developing functional ways of dealing with my emotions). He also knew about The Meadows and was very keen for me to look into their program as it seemed to fit my situation and he felt that their approach to dealing with the deep-rooted trauma might be incredibly powerful for me.

I kept up the cycle. I kept up the deception. I lived a double life and it started to affect every relationship in my life. I did not have enough time to give everyone. This relationship was requiring way too much time and even when I tried to avoid the chats, I couldn't end it completely. I even asked Simon to end it for me but as much as he wanted it all to stop, he knew that I was the one that needed to get to the place where I did it myself.

My depression got worse. I began to lose energy and not enjoy my days. I missed my outings with the kids. I began taking more of my anxiety medications than I was supposed to. The pills helped me sleep and escape all of this pain for a while. This went on for several months and I was starting to seriously think about ending my life again. I had not felt this way in so many years. Just those thoughts alone made me feel guilty because I had fought and won two types of cancer and felt like I was devaluing the gift of my life. But I was powerless over the addiction to this relationship and to the overpowering shame that drove my need.

While at one of my psychiatrist appointments, I told him how hopeless I felt. I did not tell him about the pill abuse but I know he was getting to a point where whatever we tried was not working. He suggested that I might want to take a leap and go to The Meadows and get it all dealt with at once rather than week-by-week therapy of different sorts.

It was a 45-day residential facility and though the thought of being an inpatient for 45 days scared the Hell out of me, I began to think it was my only option at this point. I did not believe I would be alive in a month if I did not get help.

Again, I felt that I had hit my 'rock bottom'. My depression was out of control, the effects of abusing my pills were evident in my mood and my isolation. I was distanced from my family and in a relationship with someone I did not want and which could cost me Simon. Again, I was wrong – this was bad enough to cause me to make the most beneficial decision of my life but it was still not my rock bottom.

One factor that was not clear to anyone at the time was that I was also suffering from issues arising from the use of benzodiazepines. My psychiatrist had put me on Xanax to help with the growing anxiety and, as it turned out later, I do not have a good reaction to any of the benzodiazepines nor any drug that acts in the same way. It was not until much later that the true danger of this reaction would become apparent.

Chapter 16

"One of the things you learn in rehab is that you're responsible for your own actions."

Dr. Dale Archer

The Meadows

A date for my admission to The Meadows was set for two weeks out – 2 November 2014, just three days after my 55th Birthday. The days leading up to it were incredibly difficult. I felt an incredible tornado of emotions – I wanted to run away and hide, I was petrified of losing the relationship (even though I had by then pretty much ended contact, I had not made the full emotional break from the addiction), I was very afraid of losing control over my medications (having someone managing my pills meant that I would not be able to have them 'in case' things got too difficult and I needed to escape) and I was scared of being apart from Simon. Although my issues had placed an incredible stress upon our relationship, he had not budged an inch and I felt our love as a constant strength throughout even the darkest moments.

We both felt that we were doing the right thing. However scary the thought of The Meadows was, I was clearly not living a functional life. My depression and anxiety were in control and it was all I could do to get through each day (which I only managed by sleeping every afternoon away and relying on glasses of champagne to lift me enough to get through). If I could finally find peace from the demons of my past, I might actually be able to find happiness – something that I had never believed could happen.

The Meadows is not inexpensive and requires full payment up front before the treatment begins. Even though we expected some reimbursement from our insurance, we had to be creative in finding ways to pay for it. In the end, we took out a loan for the cost.

On the Sunday of the day I went in, Simon dropped me off at the facility and, after one last hug, had to leave me. There was some paperwork to be done, a physical check-in and a search through all of my belongings (The Meadows maintains strict control over what the in-patient community can and cannot have while at the facility). After the intake process, I was taken to the 'nursery' where newly admitted patients spent the first few days. This gave the staff the chance to monitor me more closely and to let me stabilize enough to undertake the program with the community. I shared my room with two other ladies and I felt safer than I had done for some time. It was nothing like the facilities I had spent time in earlier – this was a calm and supportive environment and I felt relief at being there. Of course, my shyness kept me as isolated as I could be, but after a while, even that dropped away.

Recovery

At The Meadows, my day started early – no more staying in bed all day. I was required to attend meetings, group sessions, lectures and workshops but in every spare moment, you could find me isolating in my room.

It was very hard work. The Meadows bases its treatment on the concept that you have to understand how you get to where you are, what your emotional development was like as a child and how you dealt with dysfunction and trauma in your family of origin. We learned about the impacts of emotional immaturity and I began to understand that if I was to be able to live a functional life as an adult, I needed to take charge and protect my Inner Child – the girl who was still suffering the effects of the abuse – teaching her how to behave and establish good boundaries. I needed to be the adult!

One of the things that made a huge impact on me was the teaching about the way the brain processes traumatic events. I had always assumed that I was somehow 'different' or 'deficient' but I began to learn that the way I am was the brain's natural reaction to what happened. We form our behavior and our emotional facets through learning and we form neural pathways throughout our life and these dictate how we react to different situations. The most amazing thing is that the brain can relearn. Although it takes at least 90 days, with enough practice and repetition, you can actually retrain your brain to react differently to triggers. Wow! Perhaps I really could become 'normal'.

It was not all education. To get at the underlying trauma, shame and experience, we had to document our personal histories and identify all of the abuses and traumas we suffered. We then had to present these in a group setting which was one of the most difficult emotional things I have ever done. Giving voice to the abuse made it visible to everyone and I was consumed with fear and shame. I talked about details of the sexual abuse and the rape, and at the end of it all; these wonderful people accepted me and cared about me. It was and remains the most powerful experience I have ever had.

Two weeks into the program, I attended the Survivor's Workshop. This is a key part of The Meadows program and is an incredibly powerful process. Using experiential techniques, I was able to confront the very deepest trauma memories and face my abusers as an adult. It was the most exhausting and the most emotional week I had ever spent. It was also incredibly healing and started me on the healthy road to recovery.

The program also included a Family Week that Simon attended with me. There was a lot of education and also a focus on how my behavior had affected people around me. We worked through some really helpful communication techniques and I felt very secure knowing that we were together as I faced my recovery.

In the 45 days at The Meadows, I met some of the most amazing people and I slowly began to trust and involve myself more in the program that dealt with the underlying trauma that causes the depression, the pill taking, the addictions and other behaviors that are so self-destructive. These people literally saved my life.

My Meadows therapist was a wonderful, caring woman and she explained Love Addiction to me and how it wasn't the real me. As we explored it, we discovered that what had triggered these emotions was my granddaughter turning 4 years old. That was the age that I was first abused by my father. Things started to make sense and I began to feel less guilty and better about myself. She helped me end the relationship that had been disrupting my life for the last few years and though it felt so scary and I still missed those conversations, I had support and began to heal and deal with the pain.

After 45 days, I was ready to go home. It was right before Christmas 2014 and I felt like a much healthier version of myself when I left, armed with so many tools and resources that would help me continue my recovery. At the same time, it was also very scary leaving such a supportive and safe environment and I was sad to be leaving my new family.

Being home was amazing. Simon had decorated the house for Christmas and had put up a beautiful tree. He also had a big surprise for me, and when I walked in, I started crying tears of happiness. He had converted one of our rooms to a sewing/craft room. I had talked about wanting to get back into sewing and he made a place where I could walk right back into it. Spending Christmas with my family felt like a gift I would never ever take for granted again.

The Meadows gave me three wonderful gifts. Firstly, I learned so much about how I became the person I am, how Childhood Sexual Abuse dominated my emotional development and caused my brain to learn dysfunctional ways of coping. Secondly, the program armed me with tools to be able to start functioning as a healthy adult. Setting boundaries, communicating and learning to 'retrain' my brain through repeating healthy steps. Thirdly, the people I got to know at The Meadows continue to be my strongest friends and support system. I have learned to trust them and we feel a kinship that I had never felt before. I had shared my most painful traumas with these people and they had shared theirs with me. That is a connection that you don't often get the privilege of having and it was and still is a gift for which I am grateful beyond words. They know who they are and they know that I love them as my true family.

Chapter 17

"Killing oneself is, anyway, a misnomer. We don't kill ourselves. We are simply defeated by the long, hard struggle to stay alive. When somebody dies after a long illness, people are apt to say, with a note of approval, "he fought so hard." And they are inclined to think, about a suicide, that no fight was involved, that somebody simply gave up. This is quite wrong."

Sally Brampton, *Shoot the Damn Dog: A Memoir of Depression*

IOP

Although 45 days of in-patient care at The Meadows achieves an enormous amount of healing, recovery really only starts when you get out! When I left The Meadows, my ongoing care was recommended as coming from an Intensive Outpatient Program. I was very willing to do this and did not want to lose the recovery momentum I had gained at The Meadows, but there wasn't a local IOP program that I truly felt comfortable with. I knew that The Meadows was opening one up near where we lived in February 2015 and I figured I could manage with my personal therapy until then.

I also had a small group of people from The Meadows who I had become close with while we were there and we formed a supportive communication thread where we could all share and feel we were understood. We all felt a strong sense of grief at leaving the 'safety' of The Meadows and we leaned on each other for love and support.

I called the Director of the IOP every week to keep in touch about the completion date of The Meadows facility but towards the middle of February, I began to struggle a bit. It was becoming difficult to keep up the affirmations and go to therapy appointments. I began to feel a bit overwhelmed and wasn't sleeping. My psychiatrist started me back on Xanax (which had been taken away from me at The Meadows) so that I could get some respite from the anxiety and the insomnia. The Xanax did not help me sleep so after seeing my psychiatrist again, I was switched to Klonopin. Both are benzodiazepines.

At that time, I was still not aware of my adverse reaction to benzodiazepines. Although I knew that The Meadows would not support their use because of their experience of the potential effects upon addictive behavior, I had no idea that

Xanax or Klonopin could actually be a contributing barrier to my emotional ability to survive.

Finally, the IOP opened and I was one of the first three to be enrolled (I have the t-shirt to prove it!). I was so happy to go to the first session. The program was 4 days a week, 3 hours per day for 8 weeks. During the first week, we shared our stories and it felt like it was going to be a good program – it was founded upon the same materials as The Meadows but was focused on surviving in the real world. It was my reason to get up every morning and it felt like a smaller version of The Meadows and I needed it desperately.

I was unprepared for how I felt that first weekend after the IOP started. I had been so hopeful about the program, but at the same time, I was feeling a lot of anxiety followed by intense suicidal feelings that seemed to come out of the blue. I did not seem to be able to control them. I lay in bed that Friday night awake, thinking that I needed to die. I took a couple extra Klonopin pills to put me to sleep.

On Saturday, the feeling was there inside of me, blurring my judgment. I mentioned the sudden suicidal feelings to Simon and when he looked up the side effects of the Klonopin, we were shocked to see that one of the warnings was about suicidal ideations. I called my psychiatrist to ask about the medication and explain how I was feeling. He was not able to answer and so I left a voicemail.

Road trip and triggers

I missed the second week of IOP. Our son and his wife were visiting from England and we decided to take a week off and take a road trip. We drove west to Palm Springs and from there on to Santa Barbara before heading up the coast to San Francisco for a few days.

On prior trips, I had found it difficult to stay engaged in all of the things that the others wanted to do and I would often not join in. I would find reasons to take a nap in the afternoon rather than be part of whatever everyone was doing. I was eager to try out my new-found strength and I forced myself to take part in everything. If Simon and the kids wanted to walk on the beach or play a game in the car, I would make myself go with them (and, of course, I enjoyed it!).

We had a great time – it was fun and a real break for us all.

On the way back to Arizona, we stopped at Farrell's Ice Cream Parlor in Santa Clarita so that I could show everyone where I had gone for my 16th Birthday party. My friend from the Church and her parents had taken me there and it was the first time that I had had a real Birthday treat. It was a good memory.

As I told the others about my Sweet Sixteen party, I sat eating the same ice cream I had all those years ago and, without warning, my emotions just poured out of me and I cried uncontrollably. I think it was a combination of the emotional weariness of forcing myself to be 'present' for the road trip (which was absolutely wonderful, just more tiring than usual) and the triggering of deep memories that had been exposed by my work at The Meadows. Whatever the cause, I experienced very real feelings that seemed to evoke exactly how I had felt when I was 16 years old – afraid of the abuse and struggling to break free from the grips of the dysfunction that was my family.

Simon and the kids were nothing but supportive and we did enjoy the rest of the trip but the trigger had reached deep into my soul and I was scared at how easily I could feel the same feelings and have no way to stop them.

Learning how to handle the impacts of triggers is an important part of recovery. At The Meadows, I learned that we cannot avoid all triggers but that we have to retrain our brain to react differently. After a year, I still find myself triggered but I am starting to notice that I no longer become completely paralyzed by the emotion and that, although it can still affect me, I do not stay in the dark places for anywhere near as long as I did. My brain really is re-learning.

Rock bottom

The day after we got home from the road trip, I felt overwhelmed by the emotions. In reality, I was still very raw from coming out of The Meadows and the episode at the ice cream parlor had affected me deeply. I felt deeply depressed and isolated. From my bed, I could see Simon and the kids having a fun outdoor day, swimming and lounging in the sun. I watched them from inside thinking I would never be able to feel that kind of ease with the world and enjoy the simple happiness of living. I took a few more pills (Klonopin) and slept for a while.

I woke up in the mid-afternoon and I felt relaxed enough to make an effort to go outside. I poured a glass of champagne and went to sit on the patio. I thought that I was feeling too much so I went in to take a couple more pills and realized there were only a couple left.

I was starting to feel a bit woozy and as I was about to take another drink of champagne, my phone rang. It was my psychiatrist responding to the voicemail that I had left before the road trip (expressing my concern at the effect of the Klonopin) and I wanted to ignore it but something made me answer it. I was talking to him and though I didn't realize it, he could tell by my voice that I was not right. Afterwards, he told me that I had been almost incoherent but I had managed to admit to him that I had taken almost a full bottle of Klonopin. He asked to talk to Simon, who reacted instantly and, within the hour, I was in the hospital with a guard at my room.

After 48 hours, when I was physically stable, I was admitted to the secure Behavioral Health Unit of the hospital. As it turned out, I was to be there for seven days as they monitored my withdrawal from the Klonopin. They told us that if I had not taken the phone call and had drunk that glass of champagne, I probably would have died.

The overdose of Klonopin marks the lowest point of my life. It is hard to put into words the overwhelming hopelessness and the agony of the feelings that enveloped me after the road trip. I believe it was the emotional equivalent of a perfect storm – I was very delicate after The Meadows, I had reopened my story at the IOP, I was triggered deeply by places we went on the road trip, I was exhausted and I was probably on the worst possible drug for my survival.

This then, was my rock bottom.

Although I have no memory of having written it, I left a note for Simon after I took the last of the Klonopin. Whether I expected to die or not, I have no idea, but this was the first time I had ever left a note. Reading it now fills me with deep emotion and reminds me of the incredible feelings of hurt and being lost.

Simon,

I want you to know that whatever happens to me is in no way because of you or any of our children. I survived a lot of crap and I think my survival instincts kept me safe for a very long time. Letting go of these and trying to learn new ways to be has been way too difficult. More difficult than the actual abuse.

I love you and the kids more than anything in the entire world and have been blessed with so many wonderful people who care genuinely about my health and my recovery.

If I don't make it, it was not because of any of you but because of my shitty Dad and my crazy family.

Wherever there is after here if there is anything, I will be looking out for all of you and the love I have for you will never end. Ever. You are everything to me and though I may not show it as much as you, you are loved more than anyone ever in the world. I could never thank you for you and for being mine and choosing me and seeing past my faults.

I love you and any mistake I've ever made or said means nothing - all that's ever mattered to me is you forever.

I love you beyond love.

Your JJ

XXXXXXXXXXXXXXXXXXXXXXXXX

Chapter 18

"Maybe you are searching among the branches, for what only appears in the roots."

Rumi

The 3 R's - Recovery, Recovery, Recovery

The only good thing about hitting the very lowest point is that there is only one direction to go. As Winston Churchill said, "If you're going through Hell, keep going."

The week I spent in the Behavioral Health Unit saved and started to change my life. They took me off the Klonopin immediately and commenced very close observation as the effects of withdrawing can be significant and take some time to manifest themselves. Since that fateful day, I have not taken any more benzodiazepines and I intend to refuse to do so ever again.

The most amazing change started to take place. As I sat in this institutional setting and listened to others sharing their stories and their pain in the group meetings, I found myself reflecting on my entire life. It was as if all of the trauma work and the unburdening of years of shame had finally allowed me to see clearly that the adult I had become was still being impacted by the sexual abuse I had suffered as a child and by the dysfunction of my family situation.

I began to realize that I could change it and that I did not have to surrender my happiness to my abusers for the rest of my life. All I needed to know was how to do it!

Simon came twice every day to visit and relayed messages of support of me from all of my new Meadows family. It made me feel so loved and 'unjudged' that I was determined to pick myself up again and get through this. I learned to reach out to them when I was feeling down. I was never rejected. I was never judged. I was part of something so supportive and loving that I could not fail.

One of the conditions for being accepted back to IOP when I got out of the hospital was that I would have to commit to stay in a structured living environment with other women while attending the remainder of the program. I was not happy about it, but in retrospect, I needed that structured setting very much at that time. Recovery – especially the early stages – is about retraining your life and it is important to have a stable and supportive environment around you. Although I had a support at home, there were too many triggers, too many memories of simply sitting in the same spot all day, burying myself in my laptop or going to bed for hours at a time because I was 'exhausted'. Isolation is a very real threat to recovery.

I attended IOP every day and went to every group and meeting I could find – Pills Anonymous (PA), Codependents Anonymous (CODA), Adult Children of Alcoholics (ACA). I worked hard and I learned even more tools to continue my recovery.

I learned that one of the most powerful ways to heal is by helping others and giving back. I started hearing people telling me that they found my story inspiring and that they thought I was 'brave'. All of my life I have shunned any such attention or praise but it was starting to dawn on me that perhaps my story really could help other people. If I could feel that my pain and suffering would help someone else realize that they are not alone, that they are not 'weird' and that there truly is a way to get through…then I could see that perhaps all of my experience had been worth it after all.

Home sweet home

When the IOP finished, it was time to leave the safety of the structured living and go home. As the day neared, I was nervous that I would not be able to sustain the good things I was doing to fuel my recovery.

I still felt the support of everyone around me. I felt the love and acceptance from Simon and my little Meadows family. We stayed in touch and we gave each other affirmations, strength, love and acceptance – no matter what. We had all been there and there was nothing you could not talk about. To this day, they are my family. I feel as if I could reach out to any one of them at any time, day or night, and they would be there. I have always felt alone in my life but now, when I got into a bad place emotionally, I knew they were there and even the times when I did not end up reaching out, just the fact that I knew they were there got me through it.

I try. I use my tools. I reach out. I fall down but I get back up again. I trusted and nurtured some very close and healthy friendships, which I maintain today. I am not only alive, I am living and I am enjoying my life. I have a family that I love and who loves me and although not all of them are blood-related, they are closer family than my blood relatives. I see my grandchildren growing into happy and healthy people.

Because the lies of my abuse had been so embedded in my heart, it had never occurred to me that so many of the things I believed about myself were simply **NOT TRUE**. When this light began to turn on – not only in my mind but, more importantly, in my heart – it began to change everything.

Love and truth continued to enter my heart and began replacing those nasty, awful lies I'd always believed about myself. I finally recognized that the truth about me is that I possess infinite worth. I am learning that I have innate value and there's absolutely nothing anyone can do to change this. Nothing.

I am still working on forgiveness. I now understand that we forgive not to absolve those who have wronged us but to free ourselves from the burden. I am far from perfect but I know that the more I can forgive and the more that I can let go, the freer I will become.

I read once "Freedom is what we do with what's been done to us." It is not the circumstances of our lives that matter. It is what we choose to do with them. I choose forgiveness and love and I know I will then be safe and happier.

With a year gone since leaving The Meadows, I have one purpose in my life – to share my story. I am hopeful that not only will it be cathartic for me but will also give the nightmare that was my childhood some positive purpose in this life. My power was taken away from me as a young child but now I am an adult. It has been a painful journey to where I am and who I am today but I will not give my abusers any more power over me. By using what happened to me to help others either prevent or heal from the pain of Childhood Sexual Abuse, I am reclaiming my power.

I am enough.

Part Three Footnote

I never had the opportunity to confront my Dad about what he did and allowed to be done to me as a child. Even if I had, I am not sure that I would have been able to because I would have been too scared. Even looking at him filled me with shame and after leaving home at 17, I never spoke a word to him again. When I finished my first rounds of therapy, I was finally able to put some of what I wanted to say to my Dad in a letter.

Dad,

    Did you love me? Why do I care? Were you proud of my accomplishments, or more importantly, were you proud to have me as your daughter? When I was a little girl, you were the most handsome man in the whole world. I remember wanting your love and approval; somehow it was the most important thing in the world for me to know you loved me, thought I was your pretty girl, and that you were proud of me.

    I remember sitting on Mom's lap one afternoon when you had come home from work after overhearing a conversation you had with her and asking Mom if you were going to be ok after being "fired" from your job. I had a vision of someone burning you and it was unbearable to thing that anyone would hurt you - I loved you so much.

    I remember being jealous of your attention to Mom when I was very young - I wanted to be the center of your attention and love. What happened? What did I do wrong? What made you stop loving me? What made you say the things and do the things that you did to me? Was I that bad? I tried to be perfect. I tried to never make mistakes. I tried to do whatever you wanted me to do or whatever I thought you would want me to do.

    Over the years, my admiration of you turned to hate. How could I continue to love you and be rejected, humiliated, abused and disappointed over and over again? It hurt too much. My only choice was to hate you. If I didn't care about you, then your rejection wouldn't hurt as badly.

Unfortunately it didn't always work. The words would still cut into my heart like a knife, cutting until I was raw and bleeding inside. Of course, deep in my soul I knew that somehow I was doing something wrong. I was too ugly, or too tall, or too emotional, or too sensitive, or too crazy... otherwise you would be able to love me and be proud of me.

You must have had some legitimate reason to call me the things you called me, do the things you did to me, and say the things you did to me. After all your family is your life - they tell you the truth. When my teachers told me they thought I had potential, of course I knew they just couldn't see inside to the real me. They only saw the child that I presented to the world, a child with no problems, a child whose parents loved her and nourished her. Others' words of encouragement were to me a dream of how I wished I could be, but I was sure that I was no good inside - otherwise you would have loved me.

You were so tall and strong! I thought that nobody would ever be able to hurt me with you near me. I trusted you with a child's trust, which is the most innocent and pure type. Knowing that you loved me and would always protect me. When you watched while your drug dealer raped me, when the tiny spark of trust and hope left was broken into pieces, what could I do except pretend that it was still intact? How could I ever feel safe if my own protector and hero was the person who hurt me the most? The only option was to forget that you hurt me. It was too horrible to never be able to feel secure or safe.

I built a "perfect" family in my mind. I stuffed the pieces of this fantasy into a place in my mind and when a piece of the fantasy would begin to come loose and threaten to lose its place, I forced it back. I needed that fantasy family to survive; to be able to get up every day and face the unknown terrors that might happen that day. When a friend would talk about his/her family, I would file it away to be used in my fantasy. After all, I had no real firsthand knowledge of what a family was. Over the years, I gathered many pieces

171

to be stuffed into that portion of my mind so that I could recall it when I needed to forget the reality of what really happened in our family.

Of course, it has taken me a few years to even be able to think of these truths. I was very successful at creating a world around me, which did not include any memories of the hurt and betrayal you gave me. When Jack, the kids and I went to visit Mom one vacation after my brother killed himself we were going through photo albums. I came across a picture of you and me, which Mom seemed to instinctively know that I wanted to keep. It was a picture of me holding on to your hand, smiling on Christmas day when I was 4 years old. I remember the picture being taken. Someone was going to take yours and Mom's photo and I begged to be in the photo with you. Mom ended up taking a picture of me with you. What strikes me about that picture is the obvious love, pride and admiration I had for you. Mom gave me the photo and I have kept it over the years. I wonder why? Am I still trying to hold on to the fantasy that you really did love me? Am I too afraid to let the reality of what you did to me hit home? I am really not sure. I know that I have not been able to look at that picture for a very long time.

Thank God that Mom really did love me and that I felt it. She lost her temper with me and hit me at times when she was drunk. I would always feel like I could never do enough for her, but somehow deep inside I knew that she really loved me. I felt sorry for her and wanted to take care of her and protect her from you. I know now that my relationship with Mom was not healthy either, and I am trying to get to a point where I don't blame myself for things that were out of my control, but at least I know she really loved me inside. She was proud of me. If I had not felt that, I don't know that I would have survived as long as I have. As I write that, I can hear you saying, "What are you whining about? You don't have it as bad as some! What about the poor people in the concentration camps? You are so emotional!" Well...all that may be true but I had feelings and they were stomped on and discarded so many times that now, as an adult, I am not able to feel that I am worthy of anyone's love or concern. If you had killed me physically, it would have been easier than what you took from me emotionally.

Mom was my only link to my feeling any kind of understanding. I felt she was the only person in the world who would really care about the real me. You can't even imagine what I went through when she died. I had flown down to be with her, after finally being told how ill she was. The morning she died I was in the hospital with her. I showed her pictures of all her grandchildren and tried to encourage her to fight to get well. She was not aware that if she survived, she would be on a respirator for the rest of her life. I was chosen as the person to inform her of that. I didn't care if she was hooked up to a machine or not, I was ready to commit the rest of my life to taking care of her, just to have her here.

When I left her that morning she seemed so peaceful that I really thought she would have the strength to fight and recover. I had an appetite for the first time in weeks. By the time I got to the house, the hospital had called saying she had passed away. I had a breakdown. I walked around in a stupor for days.

A few weeks later after going back home, Jack forced me to call a therapist or he said he would divorce me. I was so scared to go see anyone, because I knew they would confirm one of two things - either that I was crazy or that my problems were not worth listening to and I should just stop whining. After all, that is what you had told me so many times. It was imbedded in my brain. But something happened that actually shocked me. He actually listened to me and asked questions!! I couldn't believe that he felt I was worth listening to. I had been sure he would tell me that my problems were nothing compared to others. I remember leaving, feeling a little scared and not really knowing why, but also leaving with a very unfamiliar feeling - someone cared enough to listen to me. That day began a discovery/recovery process of my memories of childhood that have to

173

date been the most painful experience of my life as an adult.

"What names were you called?" "Whore, slut etc.", I replied as if they were just the usual names a father would call his daughter. It was unbelievably painful when I began to allow myself to even think about the real family I grew up in. Once someone who seemed to really care about what I had to say and listened to me, the memories began flooding my mind. All the pieces of the fantasy began pushing their way out and were replaced by the "real" family.

Do you know how much you hurt me when you would make promises to take us to the park and then you would go out and not show up until late in the evening after you were drunk? We would pack up a lunch, get the blankets ready, get dressed and wait and wait and wait. I would always be the last one to believe that you would come. Far after it was obvious you were not coming, I would think to myself that you would be home soon and that you wouldn't forget about us.

Then night would come and the fear would begin. Not disappointment over the fact that you hadn't shown up - that would be gone - but the fear of what would happen when you came home drunk. Would you beat Mom up? Would I need to protect the smaller kids? Would I need to protect Mom? Would I be the victim tonight? God the waiting was the worst. (too emotional to finish this letter)

I never knew anything about my Dad's own past – we were not the kind of family that talked about our background. Several years after his death, I received a letter from his sister, in which she explains some of what he went through. In the letter, she tells me how she had known about my Dad abusing my brother, Ryan, but not about me. She related the story of her and my Dad's childhood which was incredibly difficult. Their Dad (my grandfather) was incredibly abusive to their Mom and would beat her frequently in front of the children. Her Mom had told her that when she came home from the hospital after giving birth to my aunt, her husband forced her to have sex with a stranger for $100.

After a string of different men in their mother's life, many of whom were physically violent, my Dad was forced to leave home at 15 years old. He lived under the pier with some very bad people. My aunt was raped by the same man who had made my Dad leave.

After a series of crimes, my Dad was given the choice of prison or the Navy and he chose the latter, only to be dishonorably discharged for drug abuse. My aunt told how he had always suffered bouts of depression and this had prevented him from holding down a steady job. When I was born, he was apparently very proud and would tell people to "look at this beautiful little girl I made".

My aunt said that she believed my Dad turned to booze and drugs to stop his pain.

Although his experiences cannot and must not be allowed to condone his abuse of me, it does give some insight into where the seeds of his own dysfunction were sown.

One part of this letter fills me with incredible sadness. Up until I read it, I had never been told that my Dad was proud of me. How I wish I could have heard it from him.

Epilogue

The pain that you've been feeling can't compare to the joy that's coming.

Romans chapter 8 verse 18

Two years have passed since I finished writing my story. I would love to say that since that time, I have thrived constantly, recovered completely and been happy most of the time. Unfortunately, that is not the nature of recovery from incest, rape and Childhood Sexual Abuse. It is a bumpy road to say the least.

In 2015, while I was writing this book, I felt a passion to be doing something meaningful with advocacy and went to San Diego with my friend Brad Simpson, that I had made from my stay at The Meadows in Wickenburg, to be trained to facilitate Childhood Sexual Abuse Prevention Training. After serving on the Board of Directors for an organization in Colorado that also had a mission of CSA prevention, Brad and I decided to open our own non-profit. We also became members of the RAINN Speakers Bureau (Rape, Abuse & Incest National Network) and I had the privilege of speaking at a High School about my experiences of assault and rape.

In 2016, also through RAINN's Speakers Bureau, I became involved in a profound life-changing opportunity to be a co-author in a compilation of other courageous women's stories which was published in 2017. Giving voice to my story gave me a strength that can only come from not feeling alone anymore. It gave me renewed courage to become increasingly vulnerable in sharing my story and growing my own non-profit to help other survivors heal.

Unfortunately, also during this time, my depression and pain seemed to be getting worse again. I started drinking alcohol every evening to take the "edge" off. I wanted to numb the painful feelings of the inevitable memories and triggers arising from the writing of my book. Alcohol would only make my depression worse but I found it was too difficult to get through a night without it. It was fast becoming a vicious cycle. I began to have suicidal thoughts again. I would get so emotionally tired. I can't even explain how tired. It would turn into physical exhaustion as well. I would feel so absolutely tired of living like this that suicide literally was the only way I could see relief.

At the beginning of 2017, I decided to try therapy again. I had not found a regular therapist since leaving the Meadows IOP in mid-2015 and I thought maybe I just needed a little support. As I look back on so many times in my life, I see that things and events have fallen into place for me in ways that can only be described as miraculous and this was another of those times. I found an amazing compassionate trauma therapist.

I found I was able to slowly open up. I was able to be honest and share the scary feelings I had inside. I could even talk about the suicidal thoughts, which I always kept to myself for fear of scaring everybody. Being able to talk about those thoughts seemed to take some of the power out of them. With support, I gave up drinking any alcohol. This was an emotionally power-packed decision because it went against everything in me to admit to being in any way like my family of origin. I didn't want to be like my Dad in any way. When I was a child, my father would go to Alcoholics Anonymous and return afterwards, drink and sexually abuse me.

In therapy, I feel encouraged and I continue to learn so much about how the trauma I experienced has affected me and I feel some hope of more healing. He holds my intense emotions with me and I am learning to tolerate these overwhelming feelings. I learned that we are social creatures and need other people. It's not enough to just speak the facts, we need to also allow ourselves to feel. For me, and many others, that is too daunting of a task to face alone. It is not always easy. There are good days and bad days. At times, I experience extremely painful 'shame attacks'. With the help of my therapist, I am developing a "Fire Drill" to go to when this happens.

The most difficult part of this journey to date is getting to know my Inner Child and learning to love that part of myself again. The little girl who blamed herself for being unlovable by the father she so desperately needed to love her, the little girl that kept the secrets. She needs me to grow her back up with love and acceptance. I find that this is the most emotionally challenging part of my recovery right now.

What I can say today is that I am alive. I am trying to make a difference in this world and I am continually learning and recovering more each day. I have a beautiful support group and when I sink into the shame, I try and remember that "I am worthy, I matter, I am whole, I am enough, I am lovable, and I always have been even when I forget."

My story isn't over yet;

I wrote a letter to myself that I try and remember to look at when I am struggling. I will close with that and the hope that everyone reading this book will take courage and hope from my words and the knowledge that we really are all worthy of love.

To Me,

I have been wrong to consistently ignore your needs and wants. I have put others' needs before yours and I have put others' beliefs about your worth over the truth of your value and your right for acceptance and love. I was also wrong to have labeled you broken, damaged, dirty and so many other negative things when you were depressed. I am willing to remember that you are a good person, even when you mess up.

I was wrong to expect perfection from you and when you failed to meet that expectation, to blame you for all the bad things that happened to you. When people don't understand your shyness, I call you unlikeable. When you try and stand up for yourself, I call you selfish. I call you lazy and unmotivated when you feel down and scared and are just trying to learn new skills. I was also wrong, during the times that you can't seem to handle the emotions that flood your heart and soul, to label you hopeless and try to stop it by stopping your life.

You don't have to be perfect to be loved. I am willing to love you as much as I can. I am willing to accept your faults and mistakes as much as possible for now and work at getting better at it. I am willing to let you accept help and compliments with grace because I know you deserve them.

Lastly, I am willing to do my best to make your needs and recovery my most important priority and continue to get the help you need for your continued growth and happiness. I will ask for help from my higher power in loving you as you are. I know I have not been able to do this in the past, but I will let my support group guide me and help me find the strength to continue.

To invite Janet to speak at your next event:

Please email: janet@janetbentley.com or
go to *www.janetbentley.com*

To follow Janet on Social Media:
Go to: *www.janetbentley.com*

To request a Childhood Sexual Abuse Prevention Training:
Please email: janet@showupforchildren.org
(Darkness to Light Stewards of Children Training)

To contact Janet for information on future books and projects:
Please email: janet@janetbentley.com

RESOURCES

CRISIS

National Suicide Prevention Lifeline: 24/7/365 call 800-273-8255
www.suicidepreventionlifeline.org

Crisis Response Network: Emergencies 24/7/365 call 602-222-9444
www.crisisnetwork.org

RAINN (Rape, Abuse and Incest National Network) 24/7/365 call
800.656.HOPE (4673)
www.rainn.org

National Child Abuse Hotline (1-800) 4-A-CHILD or 800-422-4453
www.childhelp.org/hotline

National Hotline for Crime Victims 855-4-VICTIM (855-484-2846)
www.victimsofcrime.org

CHILDHOOD SEXUAL ABUSE PREVENTION

Darkness to Light 866-FOR-LIGHT
www.d2l.org

ADULT SURVIVOR SUPPORT

SIA (Survivors of Incest Anonymous)
www.siawso.org

ACA (Adult Children of Alcoholics/Dysfunctional Families)
www.adultchildren.org

Psychology Today Therapist Directory
http://therapists.psychologytoday.com/rms/?tr=Hdr_SubBrand

Find a Somatic Experiencing Practitioner
http://www.traumahealing.org

Find Mental Health Providers/Organizations
www.helppro.com

INFORMATION AND ARTICLES

From God by Og Mandino:
www.wowzone.com/godmemo.htm

Soulsomeness - Wholesomeness of the soul
http://soulsomeness.com/index.html

Brene Brown
Vulnerability TED Talk
Listening to Shame TED Talk
www.brenebrown.com

Living Without Fear:
https://youtu.be/W_t9O5MgisM

In 2016, Janet founded a non-profit called Show Up For Children with a vision of a world where innocent children do not have to experience sexual abuse. If you would like to join us in saving a child from this epidemic, please visit us at:

www.showupforchildren.org

In 2017, Janet created a division of Show Up For Children called *Courageous Survivors*, with a mission to help heal the wounds of Childhood Sexual Abuse by providing adult survivors support, education and a platform for sharing hope and experience with others. You are not alone.

www.courageoussurvivors.com

To become a member of the *Courageous Survivors Member Group* for free, click here and enter your email:

https://courageoussurvivors.com/become-a-member.html

As a thank you for supporting me, I am pleased to be able to offer a free electronic copy of Brad Simpson's book Love Only. Click here for this amazing book of poems.

www.janetbentley.com/download.html

We can make a difference together.

Made in the USA
San Bernardino, CA
16 October 2018